*How am I Doing, God?*

*by E. Jane Mall*

Publishing House
St. Louis London

Concordia Publishing House, St. Louis, Missouri
Concordia Publishing House Ltd., London, E. C. 1
Copyright © 1973 Concordia Publishing House

*Library of Congress Catalog Card No. 72-97343*
ISBN 0-570-03150-8

MANUFACTURED IN THE UNITED STATES OF AMERICA

# Contents

# The Ecology of Me

There is so much talk these days about ecology. We have polluted the water we drink, the food we eat, the very air we breathe. It's a subject that needs to be talked about and written about. We need to be shown what we've done to the good gifts from God, and we need to be inspired to start making reparations. We need very much to read and reread the Book of Genesis and remember that God said to man, "You will dress, till, and keep the earth. You will have dominion over the earth and subdue it." We need to remember the sacred responsibility that goes with the dominion we have.

It's important, and I'm concerned. In my own small way I'm determined to do whatever I can to stop the pollution of our land. I look to the experts to tell me what's happened and to tell me what I have to do about it.

However, I'm even more concerned about the ecology of me as a child of God. He has given me life and a wonderful body and mind. How have I exercised dominion over these gifts? How have I handled the wonderful gift of life?

There are things in our world that are polluting our minds and hearts and the very souls of some of us.

So I am concerned about the ecology of me, of my spirit, and it is my hope that the women who read this book will think about their own spirits. That they will remember the times when they were less than little Christs.

This book is addressed to my sisters in Christ. The feminists and the Women's Lib people won't put it on their lists of recommended reading, but I'm not so much concerned with how to make it in a man's world or how to beat the men at their own game. This is my world too, and I have a very definite place in it. In many instances my place is a different place than that of a man, but because it's different doesn't mean it's less of a place. It is simply my place.

I can't for the life of me see anything wrong

in taking pride in being a woman and doing womanly things and thanking God for the difference.

However, don't expect this book to be one that lauds and praises the women's groups in the church who argue endlessly about potluck suppers and count the silverware and hate to give too much to missions. No, I'm not at all that kind of woman, and I don't honestly believe that any of us has to be that kind. We are capable of so much more! We don't have to be pastors and truck drivers and engineers in order to make it in this world. We can elevate our womanhood in ways that are peculiar to women. I also don't have to be unlearned and unread, knowing nothing but the latest recipe or talking about nothing but my children and their latest "cute" saying. I can be well read and informed about the world I live in. I can study my Bible with an eye toward knowing better God's will for my life. I can refuse to be involved in the petty, unlovely things that go on in the church. I can be my own person, a woman who's in the mainstream of life—but still a woman.

Yes, there are certain restrictions. But they don't concern me, because I'm not going to live long enough, even if I live to be over 100, to take advantage and make the most of all that is available to me.

The goal of the feminists, as far as I can see, is to liberate woman from her historic role as existing for the benefit of man.

Then, as Christian women who are a little confused by all this, we look at St. Paul's words concerning women's role in the church:

> There is neither male nor female; for you are all one in Christ Jesus.

But he also said, concerning women's role in the church:

> The women should keep quiet in the church meetings. They are not allowed to speak; as the Jewish law says, they must not be in charge. If they want to find out about something, they should ask their husbands at home. It is a disgraceful thing for a woman to speak in a church meeting.

And:

> I also want women to be modest and sensible about their clothes and to dress properly; not with fancy hair styles, or with gold ornaments or pearls or expensive dresses, but with good deeds, as is proper for women who claim to be religious. Women should learn in silence and all humility. I do not allow women to teach or to have authority over men; they must keep quiet.*

So where does that leave us? Some would say, "Right in the middle!" and no wiser than we were.

* Gal. 3:28 RSV; 1 Cor. 14:34-35 TEV; 1 Tim. 2:9-12 TEV.

We can't look at Paul's words and say that we'll shut our mouths, we won't teach Sunday school, and we won't braid our hair or wear any jewelry. That would be ridiculous! On the other hand, we can't ignore any part of God's Word either.

The thing we must realize is that Paul was not really speaking of women's place as much as he was talking about the quality of leadership in the church. In those early days of the church women did hold an inferior position in society. Church or no church, historically, women were inferior in the eyes of all. So they were not allowed to have an education, because this was not wasted on females. Paul was first and foremost concerned about the church. He had dedicated his life to helping those first Christians be the church, a community of saints. Elsewhere, we read that Paul instructed the people about how they should treat their brothers in Christ, how to give to the church, how to settle civil arguments. He talked to them about death and marriage and the Lord's Supper and the role of the pastor. When he talked about the women in the church, he was not so much concerned with their place or status as he was with the quality of leadership in the church. Paul certainly didn't want the church to be jeopardized by allowing unqualified leadership in it. I feel sure that everyone at that time understood what Paul was telling them and why he said what he did.

The principle, however, is as valid today as it was then. Of course, the form in which it is expressed is different in many ways, but the principle still holds true. We can't go so far as to say that the goals of the feminists are compatible with apostolic teaching, because they aren't.

Paul says the husband is the leader over the woman (Eph. 5:22). If we stop reading there, we might be inclined to say, "Women's Lib, count me in!" But if we read on, we will see that we Christian women march to the sound of a different drum.

"Husbands, love your wives in the same way that Christ loved the church and gave His life for it" (v. 25). And therein lies the difference! The husband is given a great responsibility, a heavy rap. He is to love his wife as Christ loved the church! So it behooves us, as Christian women, to try to become the kind of woman a man could love like that. We must be concerned with the ecology of our spirits, what we are as Christian women, what truths we're teaching our children.

It is my hope that as Christian women read this book, about the ways in which I wore the different hats of my life, they will try on some of their own hats again and see how well they sit on their heads.

And so, my dear sisters in Christ, this book is written for you in the hope that through reading about the errors I made and the ways in which

I ignored the ecology of me, you will stop and know of a better way for yourself.

If, like me, you've read about and been confused by the feminists and Women's Lib movements and have wondered where you stand, maybe this will help. I did a lot of reading, thinking, praying, and studying of my Bible before I came to the conclusions I have set forth here. I don't believe that this is in any way fighting Women's Lib, either. They say that woman has been held inferior, that her historic role has been to exist for the benefit of man and to accept this oppression without complaint. They want to change this.

I want to change it too! They think they can change it by not wearing a bra, by being free to commit adultery, and by being allowed to have an abortion when they want one. They demand equal pay for equal work, and they feel that women should be allowed to study for and work in any profession they choose.

That's not all of it, of course, and all of us have to agree with some of it. However, I believe that we women of the church, under Christ, can have a liberation movement of our own.

We can set about the task of liberating our spirits — of becoming concerned with the ecology of us — of trying to set our various hats a little straighter on our heads — of becoming the kind of women that all men will look to with love and respect. A woman a man can truly cherish.

The ads say, "You've come a long way, baby!" Oh yes, we've come a long way, all right! We drink and smoke and expose our bodies and have maids to clean our homes and babysitters to take care of our children. I'm not condemning this, but is this all we've got? Is this the long way we've traveled? If it is, we're only kidding ourselves that we've come a long way, that we've improved our lot. We have only made of ourselves creatures that men may like as sex objects, men may love, but certainly not women that men may cherish. So I say, let's stop putting the blame for ourselves on the men. We can be whatever we want to be, and as Christian women we should know exactly what it is we want to be. We can ignore the business about wearing or not wearing a bra and all the rest of it. We can take our Bibles in one hand and not be ashamed of the broom in the other hand and show the world that the Christian woman is a truly liberated woman in the very best sense of the word. Our slogan should be, "His way!" for we women will go about the ecology of our spirits in His way and no other way. And we aren't even one bit perturbed that this slogan for the true liberation of church women has the word *His* in it!

# I Loved You, You Know

I don't know what kind of daughter I was as a child. Quite ordinary, I suppose, since I'm a quite ordinary adult. Our family photograph album shows me as a small, chubby girl with curly hair. My hands and face were always dirty, and I usually had a wide grin on my face.

I remember incidents from my childhood: a birthday party, a broken doll, a new puppy. Mostly, though, I remember some of the talks my mother and I had after I was grown. I was in my early twenties, and she and I liked to talk about ourselves and our mistakes and triumphs, and we'd analyze them. Why had we acted in this certain way? What could we have done that would have been better? What could we do about our attitudes, our dispositions? We were amateur psychologists, all right.

I recall one time telling my mother that what I was was her fault, not mine. If I felt insecure and lacked confidence (and oh, I did!), it was all her fault, because she hadn't instilled these good things in me when I was a child. If only she hadn't been lacking in that department, I told her, I'd be a different person. Certainly I'd be a more successful person in many ways. She was to blame for this.

"These certain things about myself," I went on with the conceit and audacity of my youth, "are your fault, you know. You gave birth to me, and you raised me, and somehow there are these certain things you failed to give me."

My big mouth, impressed with its own noise, went on and on. I recalled incidents from my childhood. I remembered scraps of conversation, and I brought them all out for viewing. Many things, told from my one-sided perspective, which, I told her, proved that she had been wrong. I even told her how she could have done them better!

I don't recall my mother saying very much. She sat in her wing chair, her head bent to her sewing, the light shining on her hair. Finally she looked up, broke the thread off with her teeth, and said, "But I did the best I knew at the time. I loved you, you know." She put the thread through the eye of her needle. "I loved you very much."

That didn't impress me very much. Well, of course she loved me! I was her child, wasn't I? What kind of answer was that? I hadn't been talking about whether or not she loved me. I'd been telling her about some of the mistakes she'd made.

The years have passed, and my mother is dead. And now I have a teen-age daughter who is often thoughtless and selfish in the ways youth can be. She is also quite critical of me in some ways. "Your unlovely ways" she calls them. She doesn't hesitate to remind me of them, to call them to my attention. (Whatever happened to that little girl who looked up to me and said I was her model for being a woman? Did she have to disappear so completely?)

Not long ago my daughter and I were talking, remembering some things from her recent childhood, and she said, "Oh, I remember that time! You were so mad at me! Oh boy, I was scared because you were so mad!"

I looked at her blue eyes dancing with the memory. "I really hadn't done anything that bad," she went on; "it wasn't fair for you to be so angry with me."

I recalled the incident. She had been out on a date in her boyfriend's new car, and the roads were icy. They had come home two hours later than I expected them, and she hadn't called as she usually did.

When they had finally walked in the door, and I saw my daughter all in one piece and laughing and not killed or brought home by the police, my relief was almost more than I could bear. So I scolded her for being late and not calling me. I really had no choice. It was either retain my sanity by scolding or going to pieces with relief. So I had scolded.

I recalled all this as my daughter stood before me. I wanted to say, "But it wasn't like that at all! I wasn't really mad at you. I had been so worried and . . ." and then my own mother's words came back to me, and my words lodged in my throat.

I looked at my daughter. "Well," I said finally, "I loved you very much, you know."

She ran her fingers through her long hair. Impatience hovered behind her eyes. "Yes, I know that," she replied. "I know."

I didn't say any more, but I thought: "Oh, but you don't really know it yet, my dear daughter. Not yet. You take it for granted—as your just due. Someday you'll see it differently, as I did."

I think about my mother and our relationship. I was a good daughter, as daughters go. I loved and respected her. I had fun with her, and I let her know I enjoyed being with her.

I listened to her. Not as often as I could have, but there were many times when I went to her for advice, and I really listened to what she told me.

When she was old and alone and a little afraid of what life was going to deal next, I gathered her into my circle of love and made her know that she'd never have to be alone, that I would take care of her as long as she lived. In a way, we turned the tables, and she was my beloved child.

And then one day at the dinner table she was suddenly a stranger. She was a woman who looked like my mother with her beautiful white hair and her lovely face and warm brown eyes, but she couldn't speak, and in a very little while she couldn't see, and one side was cruelly paralyzed. In the hospital emergency room I held her in my arms and with my lips against her face told her over and over that I loved her very much. She held on to my hand, and I knew that she understood what I was telling her.

And then she was gone, and I had nothing of her but a few pictures and some inexpensive trinkets and some clothes to give to Goodwill. And I had the years and years of memories piled up inside my head.

I will always remember myself telling her that she was to blame for all the unlovely things I had become. And the memory is indelible of her soft voice cutting across my loud strident one, saying so simply, "But I loved you, you know."

I argue with myself. I tell myself that I was young when I said those things to her. And the young are selfish and thoughtless. And of course, these things are true. I don't think of this very often, just once in a while. Mostly I remember the gay, wonderful times my mother and I had together. I recall the snowy evening she and I plowed through the drifts in the dark, singing "The Music Goes Down and Around" with sound effects and a lot of laughter. I remember what a good mother she was. A loving, gentle mother with a mischievous twinkle in her eye. I see myself sitting next to her at a picnic, in church, at home. I see my head on her shoulder as I cried away some of my youthful hurts. So many things that were good and happy. I prefer to remember these.

But once in a while I remember that young, selfish girl who blamed her mother for what she felt were faults. And it's not a happy memory. It's something I'd do differently if I had the chance to do it over again. Which I never will.

My mother used to say once in a while, "You're just thoughtless."

I guess she could excuse me on those grounds. I don't excuse myself.

### DEAR GOD . . .

Well, God, we come full circle, don't we? I mean I remember my mother telling me in a sort of a laughing way that she couldn't wait until

I had children of my own. Then I'd understand a few things. She was right, too.

If I could do it all over, I'd be a better daughter. I'd be more appreciative of the really great love my mother had for me. But that opportunity is gone forever, and I have to work on what I am now. What I am now, among other things, is a mother, and I want to be a good one. Approved, in Your eyes, dear God.

I don't mean anything like teaching my children good manners or being sure their clothes are as pretty as their friends' or helping them with their homework. I mean much more than that.

I see now, partly from remembering my own mother, that the best thing I have to give my children is the absolute assurance of my love. So they'll always know it's there and that it's strong and sure. Because if they can grow up truly believing in that, it will help them know that what I say about Your love is true.

I know I'll make a lot of mistakes (You know how many I've made already!), but if I can assure them, on a day-to-day basis, that I love them and believe in them, they'll forget the mistakes I made, but they'll never forget my love for them.

You see, my children know how much I love You, God, and how very much I depend on You. They know all about the times I run crying to You and the times I can't find the words for my gratitude. They know of my joy in worshiping

You and the strength I derive from my quiet times alone with You. They know, because I tell them. I want them to have it all too.

I guess to me that's what this love is all about. You have so much of it for me — You pour it on me — and fill my heart with it, and there's only one thing I can do with it, and that's to give it away. Give it to everyone I can, and most of all to my children.

The only thing that really matters about being a mother is that Your love is multiplied. God, please, don't ever let me forget that!

I'll try, dear God, to bring a knowledge of Your love to my children, so that I can feel Your pleasure when I ask, "How am I doing, God?"

# So Where Is God?

I had a friend who always seemed to be against all the important things I believed in. We were both quite young and foolish in many ways, but I believed strongly in God's presence in my life and in going to church and in allowing God to guide my thoughts and actions. It was a very deep, positive thing about me.

She didn't believe in these things. Or at least she liked to say that she didn't.

"God? Who is He? Where is He? I was brought up in church and Sunday school, and a lot of good it did me!

"Oh, I guess I do believe there's a God—

somewhere—but He isn't here. He isn't keeping any scorecard on me personally. I could cry and scream for help, but I know there isn't anyone up there to hear me."

She said things like that, over and over. She sort of liked the sound of her own voice when she got on the subject of God and church. Still, we were good friends, and I used to ask her to go to church with me, but she would never go.

"The church is not relevant. It's out of it, can't you see that? Maybe a hundred years ago the church fulfilled a need. I guess maybe it did. But certainly not now."

I finally stopped asking her.

We worked at the same place, and when she'd get a raise and I wouldn't, she'd laugh.

"So where is your personal God? Don't tell me you haven't been praying for a raise!"

Then when I got a very nice promotion and she was still stuck in her same job, she managed to turn that around too.

"Well, you're qualified for the job. God didn't have anything to do with it. If you hadn't gone to night school and studied your head off, you wouldn't have received that promotion. God didn't have any part in it."

I gave up talking to her about how I felt, what I believed. She was my friend, and I didn't want to argue with her. Besides, I was tired of her laughing at me, making fun of my beliefs.

I don't like to think that maybe I wasn't too

sure of myself. Maybe that was part of it though. We both had good jobs and nice apartments, and things were going great for both of us. We had boyfriends and clothes and a little money in the bank.

Just because I was a Christian and depended on my faith like it was my three meals a day hadn't made that much difference in our lives— obviously. I didn't have more money in the bank than she did or a nicer boyfriend or a better apartment. If anything, she had a little more than I did.

She naturally kept reminding me of this, and it was food for thought, I have to admit.

I did think about it, and little by little, without realizing what was happening, my dependence on God grew a little weaker. Doubts crept into my thinking. Was she right after all? I pushed the thoughts and doubts away. I refused to pay attention to them, but they were always there, lurking in the background of my mind.

One day she told me that Jerry, her boyfriend, had moved into her apartment with her.

"Why not?" she answered my shocked face. "What's the difference?"

I didn't say any stilted thing about the new morality and God and morals. Instead I reminded her of her parents who lived across town. Wouldn't they be hurt?

"They're not going to know. I'm over twenty-one, and it's my business, not theirs!"

I even got up my courage finally and said something about it being immoral.

"That's your opinion, not mine," she said.

That made me angry. I was getting a little tired of her flippant, one-sided opinions.

"Not my opinion," I said, "but God's law."

She shrugged. "Okay. Let's see if He strikes me dead."

He didn't strike her dead. In fact, it actually began to look as though she'd been right. She and her boyfriend lived together, and they were obviously very happy. Her parents never found out about it. She prospered as before. As usual, she did better than I did in some ways.

My car stopped running one morning, and I had to take $75 out of my savings account to have it repaired. Her car ran fine. No problems.

She talked about the parties they went to and the new clothes she bought. When it was her birthday, her parents and an aunt and uncle sent her a total of $50. Things were going great for her—she was sitting on top of the world.

Little by little, without my being conscious of it happening, doubts crept into my mind. I kept on going to church and praying and doing what I believed in, but the absolute assurance and the joy of it were ebbing away. I wasn't that sure any longer about a personal God. I prayed, but I didn't feel as close to Him as I always had. The great feeling I'd had each morning of God and me starting the day together just wasn't in me. I kept on praying for my friend, but I was getting impatient with God. Why didn't He get busy and help her? I simply wasn't on top of it any more.

Once her boyfriend had moved in, I didn't see as much of my friend as I used to. She was too busy rushing home to him in the evenings, going out to parties, giving dinners in their apartment. At the office, she'd whiz past my desk once in a while, her step bouncy, her eyes sparkling. Over and over I said to myself, "So what? Doesn't prove a thing!" But I hated what was going on in my mind.

Then one evening she came to my apartment. The sparkle was gone from her eyes, and she didn't look like the happy, on-top-of-the-world person I was getting used to. She didn't say anything important for a long time. We talked about clothes and money and the job. I knew something was wrong though, and I tried to be patient until she decided to tell me about it.

"Is everything okay?" I asked finally.

She nodded, her long straight hair swinging with the motion. "Sure."

There was a heavy silence between us. "You don't seem as happy as you were, that's all," I said.

She looked up and there were tears in her eyes! "I feel so damned grubby," she said.

I could hardly believe her. Did she mean that her free love life that defied tradition and religion wasn't working? Had it gone sour?

"I don't really like living this way," she went on. "This sneaking, going against . . . against . . ."

"God's will?"

"I guess. Something like that. Anyway, I can't do it any longer. Freddie's moving out tonight."

We talked for a long time, my friend and I, and my spirits soared again, and I knew that peculiar joy that comes from feeling very close to God. Also, I welcomed the little rise of hope. Maybe she was changing her mind about the existence of God.

"You say it's God," she said, "but I say it's my conscience. It was simply going against the way I was raised. That can be a real hang-up, you know."

She talked on, about how it was her conscience, the fact that she was going against everything she had been taught as a child. Still, little by little, I saw that in her own way she was looking for me to prove something different to her.

It wasn't so hard after that. My strength and happiness in my faith returned to me full force. My doubts, small though they had been, were blown away like early morning fog. I did talk to my friend about the things that happen when we deliberately turn our backs on God and go our own way — against His will for us. Things like that. She didn't say anything, but for the first time she listened.

She didn't drop to her knees and start praying up a storm. And she didn't suddenly decide to start going to church with me. In fact, all she said that night was, "I'm going to go home and take a long, hot bath. See you later."

So there was certainly no big, dramatic conversion. We went on pretty much as before. There's only one change now:

She's beginning to question her own doubts, and she doesn't talk any more about how irrelevant the church is. She has never again made the statement that God isn't here. Oh, she still insists that her parents bred a conscience inside her, and going against it was more than she could stand. She says that's her hang-up and she's stuck with it.

I believe that God talked to her.

And I notice that she looks at me sometimes as though she feels that maybe, just maybe, I might have something after all. She's not quite ready to accept it for herself yet, but I've got all the time in the world!

## DEAR GOD . . .

Sometimes I get really disgusted with myself! I have known the great, wonderful joy of You for a long time now. Still, one person can come along and instill tiny doubts in me, cloud over a little of the joy. Okay, it didn't last very long, and I recovered fully, but how could it have happened at all? I've always felt that my faith was so strong and sure and I was so happy with it and no one could convince me that I could ever doubt.

I'm the one with the missionary zeal in my heart, hoping to win souls for Christ. I'm the one with absolute dependence on Your love. The one who loves worshiping You and teaching the kids about You and spending those precious moments in prayer.

I'm also the one who so quickly allowed doubts to creep in. I can hardly believe it! I didn't think it could happen to me! Now that I see how it all worked out with my friend and me, my faith has been strengthened. When the little doubts and nagging fears were washed away, my love for You emerged stronger than ever before. I'm grateful for that. It's like it had been tested, and it wavered all right, but it emerged triumphant and reinforced. I walk with a surer step now.

There's still one thing that bothers me though, God. If it happened once, couldn't it happen again? I need to think about this and be very much aware of the possibility of it, don't I?

It's odd, how you can feel so strong in your faith, and so sure, and really be working at it, and then find out you're vulnerable after all. God, I don't want to be half-safe! I want armor around my faith that no doubt can ever penetrate. Is this possible? I hope so, because so often I don't like the answer to "How am I doing, God?"

# Remember the Puppy!

When I was young, I was impetuous and impatient and quite a dramatic person. You could say I wasn't the easiest person to live with. The man I married was like that too. When we announced our engagement, friends and relatives warned us: "You two! There will be explosions. Be careful!"

But I loved my husband with a love that was almost always able to cover up the little faults and annoyances and personality differences. He loved me in the same way. Our personalities met head on at times, but usually our love was great enough to act as a buffer.

Almost from our first meeting we'd both had the same thought about each other.

"If it wasn't for you in my life, I wouldn't amount to much. You make all the difference."

"I feel the same way about you! It seems that I've become the person I was meant to be since I've had your love."

We believed that. It was true for us. We gave each other a lot of joy and happiness mostly because we were so important to each other. We might not matter to anyone else, but we certainly did to each other. It was what kept us going.

Now that he's dead I remember other things. Oh, I know it's never good to live in the past, to regret things that can't be undone or done over again. I know that. But if I can learn something important about myself by remembering, and if it can help in how I act with others, then I must remember and evaluate and use my memories for my own good.

Like the time he backed out of our driveway, over our brand new puppy, and killed it. He had just brought the puppy home, a surprise, and we had played with it and given it a name. It was our first pet, and already we loved it. When I heard his brakes screech and saw the tiny creature lying lifeless in the driveway, my reason left me.

I was frantic and I yelled and screamed at him. He didn't say much. He buried the puppy in the backyard and didn't talk about it. I was shaken and angry, and I ignored the tears in his eyes.

Worse than that, as the years passed, I reminded him of what he'd done. I'd ask him to be careful with something, and he'd mutter impatiently, "Oh, of course I'll be careful!" Then I'd say, "Oh sure! Remember the puppy!"

I'm ashamed of it, I admit. I had no right to hold that over his head. A good wife would have gone to him and cried with him and assured him that she understood his misery. It was an accident, he hadn't done it on purpose, and she would have understood that. They would have been all the closer for the little tragedy. They would have shared this unhappiness in a way only a husband and wife can.

There was another time when we were on vacation and we left our motel one morning to start the trip home. I'd asked him over and over if he was sure we had packed everything. "Are you positive everything's in the suitcase?"

Just as he was becoming really impatient with me and I knew it was time to keep quiet, I asked one more question.

"You did get my bracelet, like I asked you?"
He nodded.

"Remember, I asked you to get it out of the bathroom and put it in my little green case?"
Again he nodded.

"You're sure?" I asked again, pushing my luck.

Of course, when we arrived home and I opened the little green case, my bracelet was missing. I could envision it lying on the sink in the bathroom of the motel.

It was a very special bracelet he'd had made for me, and it had a great deal of sentimental value. It had meaning only for the two of us. I had intended to keep it forever, to give it to a daughter one day. I never saw it again. I always felt justified in reminding him of the fact that he was the one who had left it behind.

Now that he's dead the memory is bitter. Not about losing the bracelet or the puppy. I hardly remember now what either of them looked like. When I lost him, all other losses paled forever.

The bitterness is because I scolded him about something he didn't mean or want to do. About something he felt as sad over as I did. The bitterness lies in my heart, and sometimes it's very heavy.

I missed my chance, and it's too late to do anything about it now.

Except to remember it and the way I acted. And when my children do something born of carelessness or ignorance, I say to them, "You didn't mean to do it, did you?"

And I listen to their frightened, tear-filled voices saying, "No, I didn't mean to do it! I didn't mean to!"

Then I remember the puppy and the bracelet and how I acted and how I've learned since then. And I hold my child in my arms and tell him that I understand. And I help to remove his burden

34

of guilt by reassuring him of God's love and understanding. "Don't cry so," I say. "You made a mistake. We all make mistakes, and we're sorry. God knows about it, and He understands better than anyone that you didn't mean to do it." And I dry my child's tears and vow never to remind him of his mistake.

As they grow, they in turn will remember, and they'll be able to say, "You didn't mean it, did you? I'm sorry. Is there some way I can help?"

With others I meet through the rest of my life, it's easier for me to forgive and forget. On the spot. It almost comes naturally to me to say, "Oh, forget it. You didn't mean it. It's really not important." My memories help me forget my own feelings and think of how the other person feels.

Because I remember back to the times when I didn't say those things to the person I loved most in the world. Remembering, and not liking what I did and said, helps me now. A woman in the parking lot dented the fender of my car. There were tears in her eyes as she apologized over and over. I was able to comfort her and reassure her that it wasn't important. It was all right. Forget it. "You didn't mean to do it." I said. "I can see how it happened. I was parked at an angle and . . ."

Even very little things. In the supermarket a long-haired teen-age boy stepped on my toes. He apologized, but his look was defensive, daring me to scold him. I put a hand on his arm. "It's all right," I said with a smile. "You didn't mean to do it." His answering smile was warm and friendly and relieved.

In many ways, and in lots of little ways, because of a few bitter memories, I'm able to keep the peace. There are a few less frowns and angry words in my world. There is absolute forgiveness for little insults. That's keeping the peace, isn't it?

## DEAR GOD . . .

You know, God, sometimes I have very big dreams for this world. I think of what it would be like if every single one of us would always and instantly forgive every wrong. Wouldn't it be great? And wouldn't just that one thing change the world completely? Wow! It's a heady thing to think about.

If we wronged someone, he'd instantly forgive us, and we'd do all we could to make restitution. That would take care of a lot of lawsuits.

We'd all live together in such peace and harmony we'd have time for more important things.

But I'm such a dreamer, God! For some reason we think always of ourselves first and the other guy — well, maybe later. We hold grudges and refuse to forget a hurt. I did it to my dear husband; and God, I hate to admit it, but I still do it. Oh, I've learned a lot, and I really am trying to teach my children to forgive and forget, but I haven't come up all the way, have I, God?

It seems like I'm always reminding people of their past failures. What they did or didn't do last month or last year. How they forgot this or remembered that. Or how they failed to do something.

Why do I do it, God? It's certainly not Your way. You say we can be washed clean and start every day all over. I need a lot of help in remembering that.

So often I don't like the answer to "How am I doing, God?"

# Less Than a Thing of Joy

There's no doubt about it. As a mother I've done a lot of wrong things. Like yelling at my children because I was tired or busy or nervous or not really listening to them when they wanted to tell me something; or being so overprotective I confused them. Things like that. Sometimes, it seems that the best I can hope for is that I don't repeat these mistakes too often. I keep trying, anyway.

I can forgive myself for those things because I didn't really mean them and I love my children very much and they know that for sure. And as they grow and mature, each of them in turn, they get with my ways and they learn how to keep the peace. They learn to say, "Don't hit Mom with that report card right now. Wait until later." Or they grab my arm and say, "Mom! it's important! Please listen to me." When I caution them for the umpteenth time about crossing that busy street, they grin and say, "Don't worry, Mom. I'm always careful. I'll be okay." They learn, in other words, to stop me from doing some of those things I do, and it's all right. It works out well for all of us.

I think the really bad thing I've done as a mother, the times I truly regret, are the times when I've made our faith and our practicing it less than a thing of joy.

There were the times when I grumbled about going to church. Times when there was so much work to be done because of dinner guests or when there was a garden that needed weeding or when something was picking and nagging at me. Those times we went to church all right, but I don't like remembering how I acted. I yipped at the children's heels all through breakfast and getting dressed. We piled into the car, and I was grimly silent during the drive to church. Throughout the service I glanced at my watch and sighed when I saw there was to be a special number by the choir *and* a baptism that morning. I was on my way out as soon as the service was over, letting everyone know by my harried, rushed walk that I couldn't stop and chat. On the drive home I grumbled about how much I had to do and how I hoped the children would cooperate and at least not cause me any more work. Remembering these times, I wonder how my children enjoyed worshiping the Lord with gladness. I don't think I care to hear the answer to that!

And then the times when the children would kiss me good night and I'd remind them, "Don't forget your prayers." Which was fine. The times I don't like to recall are the times when one of them would come back to me and ask, "Will you come in and say my prayers with me?" I hesitated. Maybe the movie on TV was just getting interesting or I was busy with something, so I said, "Oh, come on now. You don't need me. You go on and say your prayers like a big girl." In my ignorance or selfishness or whatever it was, I missed a wonderful opportunity to pray with my child. I didn't always put them off like that, so I know what a great thing it is to kneel by your child's bed, with her little self beside you, and talk to God together. I regret terribly the times I passed those opportunities up. In the twinkling of an eye my chances were gone, and none of them ever asked me to pray with them again. Time flew so quickly, and they grew up, and grown-up children don't ask their mothers to kneel at their bedside to pray with them.

There were so many times when I'd sigh and say, "Please! Go and play. Find something to do, and leave me alone. Can't Mother ever have any time to herself?" I guess I really did have to say that sometimes. Every mother will agree with me there! But I remember a few special times when I shouldn't have said it. I missed so much! I remember a picnic one summer day. The food had been eaten and the picnic things put away. The boys had gone fishing, and the older girls had gone for a walk. Gratefully, I lay down on my back in the sweet-smelling grass and stared up at the sky. I could see white puffs of clouds through the lacy tree branches, and I was content thinking about God and me and how I was doing. I felt very close to Him. My youngest child had been left behind, and he came over to me and asked if he could lie down next to me in the grass and look at the sky and talk. The moment was a rare one in my busy life, and I wanted to hug it to myself. I didn't feel like sharing it with anyone but God. So I raised up on one elbow and said, "See that sandbox over there? Why don't you go and play in the sand and let Mother lie here alone?" I patted his dear head, but my voice dismissed him, so he went over to the sandbox without an argument. The thing is, I had something wonderful to share with my child that day, and I withheld it from him. I wish now that I would have let him lie down next to me, and we would have maybe held hands, and I would have shared with him some of the closeness to God I was feeling. And he would have talked about how he felt on that summer day and learned a little about the joy his mother had in her heart. But instead, I told him to go play, and I never had that chance again.

I can't say I've been a bad mother. Most of all, I've loved them with all my heart, and they've always known this. Together we've always gone to Sunday school and church, and we've prayed together. God has truly been the heart of our lives. I've had such great joy from watching their love and faith grow and mature into something very meaningful. They are dedicated, committed Christians with a deep love for our Savior, and I'm grateful for this. They've matured, and now their faith is personal between God and them. They're going it on their own, as it must be, and I don't have a part in it like I once did. I'm happy about this, of course, but I can't help regretting the times when I could have shared my joy with them.

I should have said, "Company or not, weeds in the garden or not, let's go to church. I wouldn't miss it for anything!" And then I should have been happy about it so that they would have seen that going to church is never a duty, never something you have to do once a week in order to keep your name on the right side of God's ledger. I should have shown them by my joy in it that you go in love and gratitude or you don't go.

There were a few times when it would have been better if we'd stayed home!

I should have grabbed every single opportunity to kneel at my child's bed and pray with her. I could have shown her what pure pleasure it was for me to share this with my child. The best book, the most thrilling TV program, could easily be abandoned for a few precious minutes of prayer with my child.

My child and I could have lain on the cool grass together and looked up at the clouds, and I could have told my child how I felt about God, what joy there was in my heart because of God. I could have told him how close I felt to our Savior and how I knew that the Lord loved me and cared for me always, and it would have been a very nice thing for my child and me.

All these opportunities are gone now, and I'll never get a chance to try again. Maybe, in the final analysis, they aren't that important. It wasn't anything cruel or hateful or bad that I did. Just some missed opportunities, but I think of how they could have enriched our lives, so I regret not taking advantage of them when I could.

It's one of the ways I'd change if I could do it all over.

## DEAR GOD . . .

You know, God, before I had children I used to watch mothers and how they acted with their children. I used to wonder why they didn't pay more attention to them. It seemed that the mothers were always saying, "Don't get dirty . . . watch your step . . . leave me alone . . . can't you find something to do? . . . go and play, for heaven's sake!" It was a great chorus that played on and on with little variation.

Remember, God, how I said that if I were ever blessed with children, I wouldn't be like that? I'd concentrate on the important things like really listening to my children and communicating with them and teaching them the great truths. Remember? I meant it too.

What happened? I did wind up with a brood of wonderful children, and I love them all so much, and I thank You again for them. But too often I join in the chorus, and I pick and nag at them and try to get them out from under foot. Not all the time, but once in a while. It hasn't hurt them, I know, but it hasn't enriched their lives one iota either! Mostly, God, I think of all those wonderful opportunities I missed. There were so many potentially beautiful times for both me and my children, and I'm so sorry I passed them up. If any more of them come my way, help me remember to grab them.

How am I doing, God?

# Count your blessings and keep your mouth shut

Because of my teen-age daughter's choice of friends I was confronted with a serious problem.

My daughter was one of the few teen-agers I knew who still brought her friends home. I was happy about this and very much afraid to do or say anything that would change it.

I'd had the turn-off treatment from my daughter and knew what it was like. I'd said the wrong thing once – about miniskirts, I believe – and I'd acted too much the mother, with too heavy a hand, and she'd turned me off, tuned me out. It had been a long road back to where we'd been, and I didn't want that to happen again.

So even though I didn't like some of her friends, I kept quiet. At least she was bringing them home, I told myself. Count your blessings!

Sometimes I'd listen to the girls talking over their constant loud music, and I didn't always like what I heard. The language some of the girls used when they thought no adult was within hearing distance was shocking. (And I'm not so easily shocked any more!)

I guess it was a combination of things. Their dress, their make-up, their talk. The way most of them were overly polite to me, with the mockery they felt barely hidden in their eyes.

There were so many times when one of them would say, "Is it okay with you if we all run down to the drugstore? We have to get something." They'd leave, my daughter with them, and I knew they had plans other than going to the drugstore. I wondered why they felt the necessity to lie to me. If they weren't planning on doing something they shouldn't be doing, why lie? But what could I do? Accuse them of not telling me the truth? They'd only look shocked and ask me why I didn't believe them, and I'd surely turn my daughter away from me. So I kept quiet.

When my daughter would return home hours later, her eyes avoiding mine, I would know that I was right. Then I'd wonder about where they'd really been, what they'd done, and always the question, "Why did they feel they had to lie to me?" However, I still kept my silence.

I talked it over with my friends who also had teen-age daughters.

"You're doing the right thing, believe me. Just keep your mouth shut."

"Be thankful she brings her friends home. At least you know they're not out smoking pot or getting drunk or something."

"That's right. Just leave it alone. If you don't, you'll be sorry."

So I listened to them, and I listened to my fearful heart, and I said nothing to my daughter.

The girl I liked the least became the constant friend of my daughter. She was in our home more than she was in her own. She ate meals with us, spent weekends with us, and she and my daughter made many mysterious trips to drugstores and the public library. This girl had her own car, so they were able to travel as far from home base as they wished.

In time, this girl started calling me Mom, and my friends envied me.

"How nice that your daughter still brings her friends home!"

"She calls you Mom? You're a lucky woman, do you know that?"

"My teen-ager barely gives me the time of day anymore."

"Mine is so sneaky! I never know what she's doing or where she is or what she's thinking.

Things have sure changed around our house since my daughter became a teen-ager."

"There's a generation gap between my daughter and me that you wouldn't believe! And your daughter brings her friends home, and one of them even calls you Mom? I say, count your blessings and keep your mouth shut!"

So I did. For a long time. Still, there were so many things about this girl that I didn't like. Vague, unspoken thoughts that bothered me, and I longed to talk to my daughter about them. I wanted so much to tell her of my doubts and fears and ask her if I was right. And if I were right, to then ask her why she was associating with this girl. I wanted to remind her of the things she'd been taught about the importance of the company you keep. I longed to talk to my daughter as a Christian mother should, warning her of the pitfalls, reminding her of things she might have forgotten. But I didn't because I was afraid of alienating her, and then where would we be?

Sometimes I wondered about what was happening to people. My father and mother had never been afraid of alienating me. When I needed to be spoken to or punished, they did their job. Of course, it would never have occurred to me to turn them off or tune them out, either. I recalled the time when I was sixteen and I'd gone against our house rules in a big way. I suppose I figured that my parents wouldn't do much to a sixteen-year-old. I felt grown up, and some of the rules were to be broken if I felt like it. My mother made me lean over her lap. "As long as you're living in this house," she said, "you will obey the rules of the family." She gave me several hard whacks that hurt my dignity more than anything else.

"Don't ever get the idea that you're too old to punish," she said. The idea of something like this happening today is almost unheard of. Still, I can't see where it hurt me or did any permanent damage to my ego. I guess the thing is, our parents weren't afraid of us. Children today know more about many things than we did, they grow up faster, and in many ways it's a good thing. I'm all for it! However, I still believe that without the leavening of a certain amount of loving control, firmly applied when necessary, we're cheating our children. They are really having to grow up the hard way.

I had never hesitated to tell my children when they were on the wrong path. I felt this was my God-given job. A lie meant punishment and a strong reminder about God's way being the only way for us. Breaking the ground rules in our home was a serious thing and not to be taken lightly. All of my children grew up knowing that if they did wrong they would be punished. I wasn't overly strict with them, but they certainly knew who was running the show!

And now I had a teen-ager, and the very word can be frightening to a parent today. The old rules and ways don't work any longer. I'd acted like a mother once. That silly thing about her miniskirts, and she'd turned me off in her new, cold, silent way. I couldn't forget that, and I didn't want it to happen again. I suppose it was very cowardly of me, but when your child is such a young teen-ager, and when you know from experience what a dark, lonely gulf that generation gap can be, you can't help but be afraid to stir things up. At least I was.

When Christmas came, my daughter's friend gave me a set of steak knives, with a note that said thank you for all the meals she'd eaten in our home. I didn't appreciate the gift. The giving of it made no difference in how I felt about her. Just as her blithely calling me "Mom" with no real feeling behind it didn't make me feel like a mom to her. Still, I smiled and thanked her and later told my daughter that it was a thoughtful thing for her friend to do.

"It was very nice of her to give me these," I said.

My daughter looked at me, the corners of her mouth pulled down, her eyes narrowed.

"She stole those steak knives," she said.

"Stole them? Are you sure?"

"Of course. I was with her when she did it. She steals a lot of things. Hardly ever pays for anything."

"How awful!"

"She's always calling me dumb because I pay for things."

I looked into my daughter's eyes and saw something I hadn't seen there in a long time.

I remembered when she was a very little girl. I had always kept a small box of pennies in the kitchen. It was handy for me for all the times when the children asked for money for gum or a Popsicle. It stayed on the counter, and every time I returned from the store I would drop my pennies into the box.

One day I'd walked into the kitchen, and my daughter was standing in front of the box, looking at it, her hands clenched at her sides.

She looked up at me with her wide, blue eyes and said, "Mom, would you put that box someplace else?"

I knew, looking at her, that temptation was proving too strong a power for her.

"I really can't see any reason to put it someplace else," I answered. "It's so handy for me right where it is."

"Well, couldn't you please put it in a drawer or something? So I don't know where it is?"

God love my dear child! I wanted very much to hide the box where I knew she couldn't find it, where temptation couldn't taunt her. However, I said no. I said that in our family we trusted one another. Then I added that I guessed I could put it in one of the drawers. And I did, while she watched me, and I closed the drawer.

"Is that better?" I asked.

"Yes," she sighed, her eyes sparkling. "That's much better! Thank you, Mom."

I remembered that, and I knew now what the question was in my teen-age daughter's eyes.

"You know, honey," I said, "I didn't know that your friend stole those knives, but I must tell you that I don't approve of her. I never have. There are things . . . "

"I know. You don't have to tell me."

She sat very still. She was waiting for something else from me. Something I knew I wasn't going to give her. Just like with my penny box, she wanted me to remove all temptation from her.

"This stealing," I continued, "you know it's wrong. Nobody has to tell you that. But I can't tell you that I forbid that girl to ever come here again or for you to be with her. This is your home too, and you have a right to bring your friends here if you want to. I will advise you to break off this friendship. It really is true, you know, that you are known by the company you keep." I stopped. My daughter was sitting opposite me with her head down, her long hair masking her face.

"Whether or not you take my advice," I went on, "is up to you. Still, I do trust you to make the right decision."

She stood up then and brushed her hair back from her face. She didn't say anything. Finally she shrugged her shoulders and left the room. It was all right, though. Her eyes had communicated a lot to me, and I had seen the tiny smile playing at the corners of her mouth.

In time, my daughter broke off that relationship. I didn't talk about it, and neither did she. The main thing was that our relationship wasn't severed or hurt in any way. I was relieved when we got through it and my daughter and I were on the same terms as before. Still, I think about it and wonder if I wasn't wrong after all. Would it have worked out even better if I'd stifled my fears and acted more like a mother right from the beginning? Obviously, my daughter had wanted something from me . . . she'd been waiting for me to talk to her like a mother, to bring into the open something of which we were both very much aware. But if I had, wouldn't she have tuned me out?

I don't know! All I can do is feel my way, learn from each experience, love her with all my heart, and pray constantly that God will keep His loving hand on my dear child.

## DEAR GOD . . .

My little girl is turning into a woman, and it's happening too fast for me! I can't keep up with her changes, God, and the gap seems to grow wider and wider. God, remember that time when she was twelve? How she cried, and I didn't know why, and finally she blurted out, "Why don't you let me wear nylons? I'm old enough! All the girls my age wear them!" We'd been at odds with each other for days, and I hadn't known why. Such a simple, easy thing it was. "Okay," I said, so relieved. "Wear nylons. I guess you really are old enough." Immediately a smile widened her face and crinkled her eyes, and she hugged me. "Oh, Mom, thank you! Thank you!"

It's never been that easy since, God. Every day gets more complicated, and I seem to understand less and less. The truth is, I'm afraid for her. She's perched on the edge of a safe nest, and she quivers with her eagerness to fly away. I understand it, God, because I went through it once too, but I'm so afraid to let her go. I can't believe she's ready yet. Not quite yet, God! She isn't fully aware of what lies out there, but I know, and it frightens me. If she could wait a little while longer, until she's just a bit older and stronger and wiser . . . but she won't. O God, I'm making so many mistakes! I don't understand very much, and it seems that I approve of even less. Will You please help me? Give me a little extra wisdom and understanding so that I can help my dear child. We both need You so much! She doesn't think she needs anyone right now, but she needs me, and she certainly needs You. So stick with us, God.

You've been keeping Your eye on us, You know how hard I'm trying, You know how very much I love You and how much I love my child. Stay with me!

How am I doing, God?

# My Brother- My Enemy

For a while I worked as a nurse's aide in a big city hospital. I made cotton swabs and changed bed linens and tried to make myself useful for a few hours each day.

A young man was brought in, and I was assigned to watch him and see that he got everything he wanted. In a few days, as we became acquainted, he told me his story. He was a detective with the city police department, and one night, while on a case, he'd been shot in the back.

They had never caught the man who did it, and the lodged bullet was killing him very slowly. I didn't understand why, but the doctors could do nothing to save his life.

I'd go into his stuffy, overheated room where he lay shivering under heavy blankets. "Read to me," he'd say, handing me his Bible. "Read anything."

I read to him every day for weeks. I prayed with him and for him. I kept asking him if he wanted some ice water, or ginger ale, or another pillow. All he ever asked of me was to turn the heat up and read the Bible to him.

Sometimes we talked about what I'd read. He was obviously a man with a great faith. There was no bitterness in him, no lashing out at the senseless thing that was killing him. He talked only of the time ahead for him, with his Savior. He was a young man lying in a hospital bed with his life ebbing away, and he was teaching me much that I needed to know.

I was young too, younger than he, and I wasn't a very gentle person. My heart too easily became filled with anger and righteous indignation. My imagination drew black and white pictures for me of what was wrong and what was right, and I didn't know how to blend them with the color of love. In his quiet, gentle way he was teaching me some things I had to know.

Soon, I knew, he'd be dead, and I'd cry and feel the useless tragedy of it. But I felt good, too, in a sad way. He was teaching me, but I was helping him. I was bringing a small measure of comfort to his last days. I was reading God's Word to him and praying a lot. I felt like a Christian should feel. Filled with compassion and pity and unselfish love.

This glorious feeling lasted until I met his wife and their two little girls. The children looked like him with his reddish, curly hair and his blue eyes. They brought colorful little drawings to show their daddy, and they were noisy kids, unaware of any need for a hushed silence. He always smiled and seemed to have more color in his cheeks when they were with him. When they were sitting on his bed, chattering, love pushed out the walls of the hot, little room.

His wife was pretty and young and much too thin. Her eyes held a haunted question that no one would ever be able to answer. I could hardly bear to look at her. Her brave little smile was a thing hurtful to watch.

It was then that I stopped feeling like a Christian. I hated the man who had done this evil thing to my friend. He was nameless and faceless, but I hated him like I'd never hated anyone in my life.

Day and night I thought about him. "Some lousy crook," I'd mutter to myself, "some lousy crook did this!" I could taste my hatred.

I recalled a Sunday school class of long ago in which we'd talked about who our brother was.

The teacher said, "Suppose a man rapes and kills the little daughter of a good man. Is that father obligated to love the murderer of his child?"

We'd all said the right thing. Of course! He had to love him and forgive him. He had to love everyone, no matter what. "Hate the sin and love the sinner," we chanted, proud of remembering that one.

I remembered that incident, and my bitterness was galling. This was different! This was real. That other had been a little horror story the teacher had dreamed up to shock us, to drag the right answers out of us. This was life as it really is, and I could feel nothing but hatred for the person who was responsible for the suffering and death of my friend. I wished he could be found and punished and I could look into his eyes just once and make him aware of my hatred for him.

Maybe my dying friend knew. I didn't talk about it to him, but somehow I guess he knew anyway. Because he reminded me of a few things I'd forgotten.During his last days he'd put the Bible aside and talk to me instead.

He talked about God's love being for everyone. And he talked about the endless forgiveness of God. And how all men are our brothers, and we must love them.

He reminded me that we are to follow Christ's example and be little Christs in the world. He talked about how Christ could hang on a cross and say, "Father, forgive them!"

He looked at me, his eyes bright. "You know, I'm at peace with myself," he said. "At peace with myself and with God."

I nodded.

He reached out and took my hand in his. His hand was cold and thin. "I have completely forgiven that man who shot me," he said. "It hasn't been an easy thing to do, but I knew that I had to, so I've been working on it." He smiled and released my hand. "I've had to ask God to help me," he continued, "and He has, and I have been able to forgive that man, whoever he is. It's given me a lot of peace."

I couldn't say anything. Tears were piling up, and I couldn't force any words past them.

"You forgive him too, don't you?" he asked me. "Because, you know, he's our brother."

In a few days my friend was dead. His body was taken away, and the little room was cleaned and aired and made ready for the next patient. His faith and his great love lived on though and brought a very special kind of peace to my heart.

That's the way I learned a very important truth. My friend was my brother, and I mourned his death. But I came to realize that the other man, the one who caused my brother's death, he too was my brother, and I had to love him also. The phrase that had seemed so inane to me, "Hate the sin and love the sinner," now held a deep meaning for me. Like it or not, that "lousy crook" was my brother, and I had to love him.

## DEAR GOD . . .

Oh boy, being a whole Christian is never easy! Like who is my brother. I have absolutely no problem with this when I go to a Lutheran church on Sunday morning and sit down and look around. Nice people. Well-dressed, clean, good people. They are all my brothers and sisters in Christ. It's easy to feel that way. In fact, every Sunday I get a very nice, warm glow, and I feel comfortable in my faith and positive of the brotherhood of man.

Then on Monday mornings I drive past a little building, and there is always a long line of men outside the door, waiting for it to open. God, they are all dirty, shuffling excuses for men. They're winos, drunks, standing in line to sell their blood for enough wine and booze money to keep them going until they are allowed to sell more blood. Every time I see them, I breathe a little prayer for them — You know, God — and I feel in my heart that they are truly my brothers. I love them, God, and I feel so sorry for them!

I know some people, God, who are just not very nice people. Rotten dispositions, stingy, gossipers who feed like vampires on other people's troubles — you name it, I've met all kinds. Still, I don't ever seem to have any trouble making brotherly love well up in my heart for all of them. I can talk to a Southern Baptist or a Roman Catholic or what-have-you and feel honestly that they are my brothers, whether or not they agree, and I love them.

No, God, my problem lies in being able to feel any love at all for those who hurt innocent people. I pick up a newspaper and look at the battered face of a child, and I feel sick. O God, how do I go about feeling love for the person who did that?

I hear about a baby dying of malnutrition because the mother was too lazy to feed it, or about the young person who tortures and kills an old man "for kicks." O God, the list is endless! You see, I know that I should feel love for these people too — simply because You do. Your dear Son invaded this world and suffered and died for them as well as for me. I know that, and I tell myself that I haven't the right not to love them. Sometimes the struggle inside myself hurts.

I'll keep trying, God. I won't give up. But I could sure use some extra help in this department. There's too much meanness and ugliness and hatred in our world, and I know that I mustn't add to it with my own hatreds. Help me, please, to feel an honest love for my brother — even when he seems to be my enemy.

Help me, so that I don't have to dread Your answer when I ask, "How am I doing, God?"

# Not Forgiving Is a Stone Wall

She was a relative, so I trusted her. Not that that makes much sense, but it was my reason then for trusting her not to hurt me.

We had been children together and had done the little sneaky things that no one knew about but us. She and I had been good friends, and since I had been the type of girl who managed to get into more trouble than the average child, I needed an advocate, and she was it.

She'd never told on me about those things, and I remembered that. They had been childish, trivial pranks, but she could have dealt me a series of little hurts by telling on me, and she never had. I don't know exactly why we feel confidence and loyalty in certain persons. Perhaps it's always made up of little, remembered things like that. We don't take into consideration, unless we're forced to, that the person may have grown up into a different being altogether.

As she and I grew and married and had families, we remained friends, caring about each other as we had when we were children. She had had a stormy marriage, two children, and a divorce, and life hadn't been easy for her for a long time. Still, she was a Christian, and her head was unbowed, and I was proud of her.

When she came to me and told me about trying to get a loan to pay her bills, I felt sorry for her. I had noticed that her children's clothes were patched and out of style. Her own wardrobe consisted of two dresses she wore over and over. I had seen the one-room apartment they lived in and had wanted to cry when I saw it. Still, she was working as a clerk in a department store, and she was proud, so I hadn't offered my help. I was afraid she would consider it charity, and I couldn't do that to her.

When she told me about trying to get a loan to pay off the creditors who were hounding her, there was a desperate look in her eyes. It shone through the pride.

I took her hand in mine. "I wish I could help you," I said.

"You can. That's why I'm here."

"I don't understand. I don't have much money."

Then she told me exactly how this large loan would get her on her feet again. How she'd be able to pay all the old bills and get the creditors off her back. How she'd be able to buy some decent school clothes for her children.

"But you'll still have that large loan to pay back," I reminded her.

She nodded. "I know. But the way they do it, they give you the money so you can pay all your bills and have some cash for clothes and things, and then you pay the loan company back. One payment each month and it comes to less per month than it would trying to pay off all the other bills."

"And will take a lot longer to pay," I said.

"Of course, but it will give me a fresh start. Don't you see?"

I nodded. "But how can I help?"

She rubbed her hands together in a gesture that had recently become characteristic.

"You know how it's been for me these past few years."

I nodded.

"I have no credit rating. The loan company won't give me a loan unless someone cosigns."

"And that's what you want me to do?"

Her eyes met mine. "Please?"

I thought about it. It was a lot of money.

I looked at her and remembered our childhood and how she'd always stood up for me and never told on me — no matter what. Of such things loyalties and love are sometimes made.

"It's an awful lot of money," I said finally.

"I know it is. But you don't have to be afraid. I'll pay every cent of it back. I promise!"

"You know what you'll do to me if you don't pay it," I told her. "They'll make me pay it, and I don't have that kind of money. When my husband was alive it might have been different, but now . . ."

"I know. It's a little crazy, me coming to a widow with four children, but I'm not asking you for anything but your signature."

She rubbed her hands together. "And your trust," she added.

So I trusted her and cosigned the note, and she got the money. I assume she paid her debts and bought clothes for her children. I didn't see her for several weeks after that night.

Several more weeks passed before a man from the loan agency called me. She hadn't made one payment on the loan, and they couldn't find her. I gave him her address, but he told me she'd moved from there some time ago and had left no forwarding address. He told me that he was sorry, but under the circumstances I'd have to pay off the loan.

It's not much good going over all the details. The fact was, I owed a lot of money, and I had to pay it. I had to pay back money I'd never seen, just because I'd trusted a relative and tried to help her.

I had considered myself fortunate because after my husband died I had enough income so that I was able to stay home with my children and be a full-time mother to them. Losing their father had left wounds that were still raw and hurting, and I thanked God that I could be there, available any time they needed me.

Now I had to go to work and leave my children in the care of someone else. In the mornings I was too rushed to listen to them, and in the evenings I was too tired to do more than kiss them good night. I didn't have time any more to listen to their childish conversations or take them on picnics or fishing trips. I went to work every day, and I was tired mentally and physically, and I missed my children. Most of all, resentment boiled inside me every month when I made out the check to the loan company.

The money represented so many things to me! First of all, it represented betrayal. It was hours of plain, hard work. It was precious time (so much of it!) away from my children. It was many other things too. But most of all it represented the betrayal of my friend.

In a little over two years I'd paid the debt, and it was over. I quit work then and stayed home with my children and prayed that they truly understood why I'd had to desert them for over two years. We tried to forget it ever happened. We said it would be one thing we'd never talk about.

I've never seen my relative again. I don't know where she is or how she is. Truthfully, I've never tried to find her. There was one time, long months after that debt had been paid, when the phone rang and I answered it, and it was she.

"I'm back in town," she said.

I said nothing.

"We've been all over the United States practically, trying to get on our feet. Trying to make a fresh start."

Still I said nothing.

"I'd like to come over," she said then. "I want to talk to you about something."

"I don't think you'd better," I said finally. "It would be best if you don't." My voice was cold.

"You don't want to see me, then."

"No," I answered, "I really don't."

She tried several times after that to get to me, but I had my ways of avoiding her, and I guess she finally gave up.

She wrote me a note asking me to forgive her for what she'd done. She offered to start paying me back, a few dollars a week. "If you would listen to me," she wrote, "and let me explain what happened, I know you'll understand."

I sent a note to her. "I'm sorry. I can't forgive you. Please leave me alone."

I've never heard from her again.

The thing is I can't feel sure in my heart about her, even yet. As far as I'm concerned, she's disappeared, and I don't suppose I'll ever see her again. I know that the cold fact of my complete unforgiveness blew across her heart, and she'll never come to me again.

I've thought so much about this over the years. I felt that, when she disappeared, leaving me with her debt to pay, knowing how difficult it would be for me, she had betrayed me. She had laid her Christianity aside for a while and had taken advantage of me. But of course, in refusing to forgive her, I was doing the same thing. In time, I asked God to forgive me for not forgiving.

I guess she knows, as we surely knew when we were children together, that I had no right to refuse her my forgiveness. Christ says we are to love and forgive over and over and over. So even though I know that she did a wrong thing to me, I didn't help matters any. I am in the wrong every bit as much as she is.


## DEAR GOD . . .

Sometimes I find myself building a wall that separates me from someone else. I deliberately lay those bricks of unforgiveness one by one, with grim self-righteousness, until it's too high to see over. I've done it more than once, and I suppose, being the way I am, I'll do it again. I don't ever want to, God. Never! Once the wall is there, I'm always sorry, and I always regret having built it. But then, somehow, it's always too late. Building it is so much easier than tearing it down.

I always say that the next time someone hurts me or cheats me or whatever, I'm going to start right at the beginning thinking thoughts of love and forgiveness. If I can do that, no one can really hurt me. Not where I live. They can ruin my name or take money from me, things like that, but if I can respond in my heart with forgiveness and a prayer for them, they can't touch me. That's always my plan, God. I think of my dear Savior hanging on a cross and saying, "Father, forgive them!" And I know in my heart that I must not do less. He expects that of me, doesn't He?

But it never seems to work out that way! As soon as someone does something hurtful or unfair to me, it's so natural for me to want to fight back. And I do, in the only way I know. Because someone cheats me, I'm not going to cheat. Or I won't repay untruths with more lies or betrayal with another betrayal. But I have another weapon, as you know, God, and it's one I use far too often. Those bricks of cold unforgiveness! And I always find myself busily piling them up, one by one, until I've walled out the other person.

So God, the only thing I can think of is to ask You to help me think less about my wounded feelings and try to think about the other person who will be on the cold side of the wall. Help me realize that maybe they're sorry and silently begging for a chance to say so. Help me see that in forgiving them and still loving them, I'll put the burden for the wrong back on their shoulders where it belongs. And that maybe, oh, maybe, dear God, both of us could arise from the experience closer to You. I know it can't be done if I build that wall. Help me, please?

If someone hurts me again or cheats me or wrongs me in some way, give me the strength I need to not build that wall of unforgiveness so that I can stop and look to You and expect a better answer when I ask, "How am I doing, God?"

# My Soul Delights in Gossip

I knew a pastor who had a wife and children and a parish. He had it made, you know, with a good salary and a modern parsonage, and a congregation that loved him. Then he started running around with a young girl in the church, and it wasn't long before the truth was out. In no time, his marriage was a shambles, his ministry was finished. All because of lust, he lost everything he held dear. He wasn't a Lutheran, thank God!

Well, I knew a priest who had a girl friend on the sly. He used to tell members of his parish that he was going fishing for a couple of days, or skiing in the mountains, or visiting his aged parents. Naturally the people in his parish never thought to doubt his word. I don't suppose anyone ever found out about the girl, but I happen to know that he spent a lot of days and weeks with her. He's still a priest, and as far as I know, he's still visiting his girl friend.

That's a Roman Catholic for you. Big talk about celibacy, but if we only knew what really goes on!

Same with the Baptists and those who preach abstinence. I could tell you some tales about that, believe me! They all drink like fish, only they're sneaky about it. I *know* what I'm talking about!

There was this young man who helped in the church. He was the perfect picture of a fine, Christian man. He always talked about how much he enjoyed serving the Lord. He'd bring the collection plates back to the sacristy every Sunday and count the money and make out the deposit slip for the bank. The pastor trusted him completely. Then it came out years later that he'd stolen money every Sunday for years. It came to quite a large amount! The pastor was shocked, but I don't know why. All these pious, sanctimonious people are like that. One thing to your face, something else behind your back.

I guess we've all been guilty of this sort of thing. I know I have. I don't know why we love to talk about the failings of people and especially about the downfall of the professed Christians. For some reason, that seems to give us a real kick.

I suppose it makes us feel better and more righteous by comparison, and that's why we drag the dirt out and spread it around. We know we're far from the ideal Christian in our lives . . . we know how often we slip . . . how badly we fail. Maybe the only way we can look good to ourselves is by comparing our lives and actions with some outstanding Christian who has slipped mightily.

I wonder why we're like this. Certainly it denotes a lack of self-confidence, and every time we drag somebody's name through the mud of gossip we admit something very unlovely about ourselves.

I indulged in this great national pastime once, and I'll never forget how ugly it made me feel. I had a friend who was known as a very religious person. She talked about it a lot. She went to church a couple of times a week and talked about that too. Frankly, there were many times when I simply got sick and tired of hearing her talk about God all the time. Sometimes I'd think to myself, "Oh, why don't you keep quiet? I'm as good a Christian as you are; I just don't talk about it all the time." Sort of like it was a contest.

Still, when I had serious problems with my

teen-age daughter, I talked to this woman about it, and she sympathized with me and gave me comfort. She was very understanding, and the fact that she kept saying, "Come on, let's take it to the Lord in prayer," didn't bother me as it usually did. We did take it to the Lord in prayer, and I was grateful for the comfort.

Through the whole mess, my friend was there beside me, offering her love and comfort, and I leaned on her. Perhaps the whole thing shouldn't have been so embarrassing to me, but it was. People necessarily knew about my trouble, and I thought their eyes were accusing.

"If you'd been a better mother, maybe this wouldn't have happened."

"Are you sure it's not your fault?"

"What is there about you that we don't know?"

I guess it was self-accusation bouncing back at me, but I felt like screaming at them, defending myself.

I knew that I had been the best mother I knew how to be. How could I know why my teen-age daughter had suddenly turned into a person I didn't recognize? I didn't know why she was doing these things that were rocking our world! I felt ashamed, and I hated it.

It's not easy when you feel you can't hold your head up to the world.

My friend was my main solace during those frightening weeks. Together we talked about

God's great love and how He cared very much about what was happening to my daughter and me. We prayed together, and I had the great comfort of knowing that she was praying for us. Instead of losing my faith altogether and maybe screaming at God for allowing it to happen, or something equally foolish, I found my dependence on Him and love for Him were strengthened because of this trial.

Some months later, my friend's young daughter abandoned her plans for college and got married instead. It happened before any of her friends knew it was even being contemplated. Very hurriedly, quietly, on a weekend, her daughter was married. None of us knew who the boy was. There was naturally a lot of whispering and guessing making the rounds.

My friend confided in me. Her daughter was pregnant and had chosen marriage to a boy she barely knew rather than disgrace. She looked at me with tear-filled eyes. "Don't tell anyone," she whispered. "Please!"

I didn't mean to gossip about my friend. She had just seen me through a very difficult time, and I didn't want to repay her friendship and kindness by hurting her.

However, I did tell just one other person. She was one who had looked most accusingly at me during my trouble. And she had held my friend up as an example of a real Christian woman. "Look at her and her daughter," she'd said. "No

trouble there, and there never will be." Insinu-
ating, I had thought, that I wasn't and could
never be the kind of Christian mother my friend
was. The old contest again!

So I guess it was jealousy that made me tell
this woman about my friend's daughter. I gave
her the scant details, refusing to elaborate or to
tell all I knew about the situation. I just made
sure that this person knew that my friend's
daughter had to get married because she was
pregnant.

I didn't say to this woman, "You see? She's
not immune. You have always said she was such
a fine Christian woman, and you compared her
to me, and I always came out second best. Because I had trouble with my child and she didn't,
you were convinced that it was because I was
a failure as a mother, and you thought my friend
was such a perfect mother. Don't deny it, I saw
it in your eyes many times. But look, she's got
very serious problems now with her child. Even
worse than mine." No, I didn't say those things
when I passed the gossip on, but I might as well
have said them. They were in my heart, prompt-
ing me.

For just one moment after I told her, I felt
better. There! The truth was out. It certainly
had taken that accusing look out of the woman's
eyes. It gave her a little food for thought, all
right. I begged her not to tell anyone. "Please,"
I said, "don't tell a soul!"

She did, of course. A great whispering campaign was conducted, and my friend's daughter and husband had to move to another state to escape the talk. My friend bore up very well. She kept her head high and went on almost as though nothing had happened. I had to turn away from the pain in her eyes. I noticed that she had stopped talking about God and her faith and her church attendance all the time. I knew she still believed, I knew that her faith hadn't been shaken, but I understood that she didn't have the heart to talk about it as much as she used to.

My friend has never accused me. She's never mentioned it to me. Still, I know that she's very much aware of who spread the story. She knows, and still she's my friend, and she doesn't accuse me.

I accuse myself!

## DEAR GOD . . .

I'm Your child, and I love You and worship You! Can You believe that I'd do anything so rotten to one of Your own? I did, as you know, and I'm so sorry. It's a very dark blot I'll carry with me as long as I live.

I can take a dress apart and make it over, turn an ugly garment into a lovely one. I can refinish old, scarred furniture so it looks like new. If I goof with a recipe, I can throw the whole mess away and start over and do it right. No sweat! But the words that come out of my mouth can't be recalled or refinished or done over in a better way. Once they're said and heard, they remain, and the results of them keep rolling on and on like the endless waves of the ocean.

I absolutely despise myself when I open my big mouth and say something that hurts another person. I try to be careful, Lord, I really do, but something gets in my way. I guess it's my ego thinking if I put someone down I'll raise myself up. I know there's no truth to that, but this unlovely, ego-centered part of me fogs the truth. I see the truth only after my big mouth has done its work.

Like this "contest" thing going between my friend and me. Because she talked so much about how great her love for You was, I wanted to prove that mine was just as great, even though I didn't talk a great faith all the time. If the truth were known, I guess I really was afraid that I wasn't nearly the Christian my friend was. Was that it, God?

Oh, I don't know, God, why I did such a hateful thing! Gossip is ugly and hurtful, and it leaves a very bad taste in my mouth. I guess my indulging in it only proves again how very much I need Your saving grace.

The next time I know something about somebody — something that shouldn't be spread around — I hope and pray I'll remember to keep it to myself. And then I'll get a better answer when I ask You, "How am I doing, God?"

# Skits and Spaghetti for God

For a long time I was a faithful, hardworking member of the women's organization in my church. I very seldom missed a meeting or a luncheon or a mother-daughter banquet. I contributed my time, talent, and treasure, and it was fine. I enjoyed it because it was more like a club than church. We put on skits and plays and musicals, and we worked very hard planning menus and programs. We put on style shows. We made money with our bazaars and luncheons and dinners. It was a lot of hard work but a lot of fun too.

Once in a while I'd feel a tiny twinge of impatience when the women would concentrate more on indoor-outdoor carpeting for the church kitchen or on flowers for a luncheon than they did on anything church-related, but for the most part I enjoyed myself for years. I was one of them, and if the pastor seemed to get a little impatient with us once in a while — well, he was fairly easy to ignore.

Then I got involved in deep, serious Bible study, and something happened to me. My faith grew, and I felt myself leaping — flying — over old walls that had held me back. Walls that had kept me from seeing certain truths I needed to see. Even though I hadn't known that at the time. For several years I immersed my mind in this study, and it did wonderful, marvelous things for me and my faith. I read about Anna, who served God with her fasting and prayers night and day; and the woman who touched Jesus' cloak, knowing that just in the touching there was healing. So many of them! Abraham's wife, who believed for so long and with so little reason for believing. Ruth, who said to her mother-in-law, "Where you go I will go." There was so much character to these women; their whole lives were dedicated to God and His will and purpose.

With all these truths and this newfound knowledge in my heart and mind, I went again to the meetings of the women of the church. They were the same, but I'd changed. I felt like a stranger. I looked at them and listened to them with new eyes and ears, and I was angry. (Righteous anger, God!)

The women discussed the fact that they hadn't given anything to benevolence in months.

"I know we should, of course, but we need to have some money in the bank, don't we?"

"It's important to maintain a healthy bank balance."

"Of course! In case of an emergency!"

"Pastor's wedding anniversary is soon. We'll have to give a tea or something."

"Right! Let's hang on to our money!"

And so they voted not to give anything to benevolence. At least not yet. My angry hand waved the only no vote. I went home muttering to myself, thinking of the widow who gave her last few pennies.

Another time they dispensed with the Bible study so they could put on a skit. A darling little thing about mothers and daughters and the generation gap.

"I know it's a little bit silly, but it does have a message if you listen for it."

"We do need to have fun once in a while, you know."

"All the girls worked very hard on this skit. Let's give them a big hand."

I sat through the skit, numbed with boredom,

furious with these foolish women. Later, I sipped coffee and munched a cookie, but I said nothing.

Later, the women worked long hours preparing for a spaghetti dinner that would put a lot of money into their treasury (to just lie there and wait for an "emergency"!), and my head whirled with their talk, talk, talk about food, food, food. Garlic bread with the spaghetti or not? What about hot rolls? Who is going to make the salad? On and on they went. Was that all they ever thought about? I wondered.

But why go on? I was disgusted, and I went home and told myself that I wouldn't be a part of them any longer. I couldn't. So I stayed home and studied my Bible and let them have their skits and spaghetti. It wasn't for me. I didn't want to have anything to do with them.

Then one day a neighbor and I were talking over a cup of coffee, and I told her about the women at the church and what they'd done and how misguided they were. This woman never attended church. She said that the women who were really "cool" didn't go to church nowadays, and they certainly wouldn't have anything to do with the women's organizations! "The church," she'd told me, "is not relevant. There's no point in going or being a part of it. Absolutely no point." I had always argued with her, but now I was beginning to wonder if she wasn't right after all. When I went to the meetings, I had to listen to talk about suppers, skits, luncheons, money, etc.

If I stayed home, I could study my Bible, so maybe my neighbor was right. The church wasn't relevant. At least the women's organizations weren't. Even the bulletins on Sundays had a lot of items about food. Luncheons, church picnics, potluck suppers, and so on. Is that all the church was concerned with? Long ago I'd heard someone say, "The Lutherans think they're going to eat their way to heaven!" Now I was beginning to wonder if this wasn't true.

When I told my neighbor about quitting the women's meetings, not going to them any more, she asked:

"But why did you stop going?"

"I just told you why! Skits, spaghetti dinners..."

"Yes, but wouldn't it be better to keep going to the meetings?"

"What do you mean? You're the one who always says it isn't 'cool' to go to those things."

"Yes, I know, but I don't think it's cool to give up either. Why quit?"

I laughed. "You sure don't understand women, do you?"

Her eyes were serious. "I don't know church women," she said, "but it seems to me that it would be better if you kept on going to the meetings and tried to shift their emphasis."

"Shift their emphasis?"

"Sure! Do your own thing. Make it interesting so they'll want to change. Get their minds off skits and spaghetti."

I didn't pay much attention to my friend. What did she know? The women of the church had been doing the same things for years and years, and I wasn't going to change them. When some of the women asked why I wasn't coming to the meetings any more, I made vague (dishonest!) excuses about how busy I was. Eventually they stopped asking me to attend. "They don't care if I attend or not," I thought; "they're perfectly satisfied with their little 'club,' and if you can't conform, you're not particularly welcome anyway." So I stayed away from their meetings. I went to church, and I'd read in the bulletin about a potluck supper and a ladies luncheon and a picnic, and I'd realize anew that I was right. They didn't have anything on their minds but food. Not for me, thank you!

I concentrated more and more on my Bible study. "This is where it's at," I told myself. "Certainly not in the food society." But still it was through my Bible study that I saw where I was wrong. One day I read about Christ storming into the temple, His eyes flashing, taking great, angry strides as He overturned tables and sent coins flying in all directions. I'd read this before, of course, but now it meant something entirely different to me. I liked this picture of Christ. The gentle Christ, holding a child in His arms, is beautiful, and so is the Christ who stops and talks and cares about a prostitute and feels pity for a widow, but this Christ who isn't afraid to show His honest, righteous anger is my Christ too. I couldn't stop thinking about Him.

He didn't peek into the temple, see what was going on, and walk away. And then sit down and tell his friends about those terrible people and say, "Well! I'll never go there again!" No, He acted in a very positive way, and He showed them where they were wrong. And when He was through, they knew a better way. Whether they went His way or not was another story, but He had told them. He hadn't kept quiet. And He hadn't forsaken them.

I remembered my friend saying that it wasn't cool to give up.

I thought about myself. How could I have acted like a little Christ, the way I'm supposed to? First of all, I had been very critical and very impatient. Who did I think I was? I needed to do some more thinking on that subject. Also, I could have tried to show those women — my sisters in Christ — where and how they could shift their emphasis. I could have worked at it, tried to come up with some interesting Bible studies, some different programs on missions. I could have tried.

And then I knew what I had to do. I had to swallow my pride, humble myself, and go back. I had to attend the meetings and work for what I was convinced was right. I had to plead, if necessary, for more interest in missions. The main thing I had to do was to stick with them and hope and pray that all of us would grow in our faith together.

## DEAR GOD . . .

Sometimes I wonder if I'll ever grow up! You certainly must have some very serious doubts about me. Like a child, I get so impatient with people. It seems that they should know better, because I do, and I can't stand to be around their ignorance. Forgive me, God.

The other day my son acted in a very unlovely way. He was trying to help his little sister with her homework. A quiet, serene picture. They were sitting at the dining room table, their heads bent over a book. Then he stood up and pushed the book away. "Don't you even know that?" he said, his voice ugly.

His sister's eyes filled with tears. "No, I don't know it," she replied. "I haven't learned that yet."

He walked away in disgust. "Then I can't help you, dumb bunny," he said.

I stepped in. "That's not the way to help your sister," I said to him. "You've been through all this; you learned it last year. You shouldn't get impatient with her because she hasn't learned it yet. Show a little patience. Help her!"

His frown started to vanish.

"Remember last year?" I reminded him. "You needed help too."

The bad feeling dissipated, and my son went

back to the dining room table. With a tiny sigh he said, "Okay, let's start over."

It took a few minutes, but eventually I got the picture, God. Not everyone is where I am in my faith. And I wasn't always where I am now. I had had to learn, and I had needed help.

So, dear God, even though I've traveled some and learned quite a lot, and even though I feel that I know some very important truths that I didn't know before, still—help me grow up! Help me realize that if I hug this newfound knowledge to myself and get impatient with those who haven't learned it yet, I haven't really learned anything at all about You.

The next time I'm with my brothers and sisters in Christ and I see that they haven't matured in their faith quite as much as they could, I hope and pray I'll have the good sense to use what I've learned about You. I want to feel nothing in my heart but love for my brothers and sisters. And, O Lord, I want to be able to look to You with confidence in a better answer when I ask, "How am I doing, God?"

# Feel, Me, Touch, Me

I was a Sunday school teacher for a good many years before I took on a class of teen-agers. I had taught the little ones, I'd taught adults, I'd been Sunday school superintendent, and I'd served as superintendent of vacation church schools several times. In other words, I was an old hand in the Sunday school.

When I was asked to teach the teen-agers, it didn't frighten me at all. Ignorance is bliss, and I prepared for my first Sunday with the new class with confidence. I outlined my lesson and made a colorful map to illustrate it. I looked up all the Biblical references and their applications. I was ready for my class of young people, armed with a textbook, a Bible, and my years of experience.

It didn't work out right from the very beginning. The teacher they'd had before me had simply let them talk about anything they wanted to talk about.

What they wanted to talk about was football games, parties, and dating.

What they didn't want to talk about was the Bible and God and the necessity of prayer.

I had thought that my predecessor was not a very good teacher. Now I suspected that she had simply given up. I felt a kinship with her, whoever she was. For a few Sundays I let the kids talk. I knew that at their age there was no parent who was going to tell them they had to go to Sunday school. If they didn't like it, they'd simply stop coming. This sure knowledge put a sort of fear into my heart.

In the midst of their chatter about boys and parties and clothes and football scores I tried to inject something about what Christ would have them do.

"Say, that story you just told about the football game reminds me of what St. Paul said once about running the race . . ."

"We talk a lot about clothes, don't we? Well,

Jesus had something to say about the lilies of the field, and . . ."

It didn't work. Their eyes turned toward me, glassy with indifference. What did that have to do with the football game? or the pretty clothes they loved?

I tried a lot of other things that didn't work. Where do you go to find ideas and material that will keep a class of teen-agers interested? I wanted them to get excited about what was in the Bible, what it had to say about God and His will for their lives. Most of the material I read was boring and pedantic. Some of it seemed to be pretty good, but I had no luck with it, and I couldn't figure out why. One time I passed around a slip of paper and asked them to write their honest reactions to Sunday school classes in general.

"They're so boring."

"Sunday school really turns me off."

"I've learned all this stuff for years. Why go over and over it?"

"I get enough of this in school all week."

I read their comments over and over, but it didn't help. I still didn't know what to do.

In time, they sensed my frantic struggle and knew that they were on top, and they tuned me out. They were polite in a sarcastic way, and most of the time I might as well not have been there. There was no communication between us. If I insisted on reading to them from the Bible, they stopped talking and sat like wooden statues until I'd finished. Then I'd say, "Shall we discuss this?" and they'd look at one another and shrug their shoulders and remain silent. If I asked them to bow their heads in prayer, they obediently lowered their heads, but I felt as though I were in a locked cell, praying all by myself.

I could have gone on for the rest of the term, letting them use the Sunday morning hour for a social gabfest. Why not? Nobody would ever know that I'd been a complete failure. The kids would never have told anyone, and, let's face it, no one in the church has ever, to my knowledge, inquired about how a Sunday school class was going. Really going. Not really inquired, wanting to know, with an offer to help. If order was being kept and enrollment and attendance noted and money collected in the wicker basket every Sunday, everything was obviously going according to schedule, and why rock the boat? Nobody would ask what the kids were learning. I could very easily let things slide along. In fact, if I did, I would sure be asked to teach the class the next term! Nobody had to know the truth.

Except me. My failure to reach these kids bothered me. In a way, I was beginning to hate them for not giving me a chance. It didn't seem fair. I'd look at their long hair falling over their eyes and their short skirts revealing so much flesh, and I'd listen to their voices having their own way, and I wanted to scream at them:

"Listen to me! Give me a chance! You're not being fair!"

But of course I didn't yell at them. They'd only look at me with that special quizzical look they reserve for those over thirty, and then they wouldn't come back the next Sunday. And I'd have to admit publicly what a failure I was.

And too, I'd always wonder what I had done that was wrong. What I could have done to make it better. It would be a dissatisfaction that would stay with me, and I'd always regret the missed opportunity. I knew that I had something to give to these young people. I had years of experience and a deep, trusting faith, and I should have been able to communicate it to them. But I decided not to do anything that would chase them away. Since I didn't know what to do to put a sparkle of interest in their eyes, I let them have their own way. At least they were there every Sunday, and my enrollment book didn't show a lot of *A*'s for absent. I didn't wonder at all about why they kept coming. This was an opportunity for them to get together with their friends, to talk over Saturday night happenings and make plans for Sunday night. It was like a club.

As the Sundays rolled by, my Christian love grew less and less. It was like a fire going out — down to the last spluttering. I hated the fact of it, what these kids were doing to me, but I felt absolutely helpless to change the situation.

Then I met a brother who turned me on to

something great. Through him the fire burned again. He's a young, with-it pastor, a creative person, a man on fire with the necessity of spreading the good news of Jesus Christ . . . of making it alive and real and relevant. His special ministry is to the youth, and he turns them on to Jesus Christ in a wonderful, exciting way.

And then I was into experiential teaching, and the miracle happened. My class of teenagers and I sat around a table on Sunday morning, and we communicated. Chatter about dates and football games wasn't as interesting as what we were doing.

One Sunday we passed an apple around. "What is there about this apple that reminds you of a family?" I asked them.

They looked at the apple and turned it over and over in their hands. They smelled it and thumped it with a snap of their fingers. They passed it on to the person next to them. Their expressions were very serious.

"Well, the skin of the apple is protective. Parents are like that."

"There are seeds inside. Like the children in a family."

"But the apple can be broken in half and the seeds exposed."

"Yeah. Like when there's a divorce."

"Or one of the parents dies."

"The apple can turn rotten. Some families do, too."

"This apple smells good. My family has a nice smell like that, too."

And on and on they went. And when they'd finished with the apple, we talked very seriously, and in depth, about parents and divorce and families that had turned rotten.

We discussed God's will for parents and their children and what a Christian family is like. We talked about a parent's responsibility to his children and what the children owe their parents.

One boy told of not being able to communicate with his father. He talked about his attempts to talk to him and how he always seemed to fail. He had tears in his eyes as he talked about it.

The other kids made suggestions. "Why don't you wait until he's not tired?"

"Why not just come right out and ask him why he won't talk to you?"

A girl told what it was like when parents divorce. She had great difficulty in spreading her love around.

Oh, how we talked! We used the apple, and then one Sunday we used a record of one of the latest rock hits and talked about what the words of the song really meant. We used puzzles and pieces of paper, and we related! We learned and grew together week after week. Instead of sitting in my teacher's chair and trying to force-feed them, I sat in a circle of love with them, and we learned and explored some truths together. We touched one another. We held hands in our circle and passed the peace. We weren't afraid to show our honest emotions.

I thanked God for using my friend, my brother, to show me an important truth: as a Sunday school teacher I am a channel for God to work through.

I had relied so much on myself and my experiences and my knowledge, and I thought the kids should welcome me with open arms. And that they should bless me for coming to them to teach them.

So I had gone to them armed with outlines and lecture notes and maps. And I started to lose my love for them when they rejected what I had to offer.

Now, as God's channel, with experiential teaching, I can take the simplest object and hold it up and ask a question, and we're off and running. God is using me, and at last I know that.


## DEAR GOD . . .

Oh, dear God, why did it take me so long to learn this great thing about communicating? And this other wonderful truth about how much we need one another. People — your creation — men and women, boys and girls, we all need one another so much. And half the time we don't even know it.

Thank You for using one of Your servants to show me how to communicate. Actually, he showed me that love is the real channel. Instead of sitting on some lofty perch and spouting great truths from the Bible and showing the kids how smart I was and how much I'd learned, I simply communicated with them. My friend taught me that it was better to care about the kids and their problems and their heartaches and then together, hands touching, to explore together what You have to say about it.

For so long I sat on my side of the generation gap and did nothing but resent the kids and breathe prayers of thanksgiving that there was a gap.

Now I see how different it really is. The kids are carrying a lot of doubts and hurts around in their hearts, and they're important feelings, not to be taken lightly. They desperately want some answers. At the least, they'd like a little comforting and assuring. They certainly don't need lofty lectures or nice little Bible stories. They are silently crying, "Feel me! Touch me! Find out where I really live, and help me!"

O God, it's wonderful that now I don't look at them with the — well, let's face it — the disgust that I once did. The boys' long hair, the girls' miniskirts and eye shadow, the bare feet of both of them, and the different language they speak, and — well, none of it impresses me in any way any longer. Because now I'm able to see through it and beyond it, and all I look at now is people.

Thank you for that, dear God, and please help

me to stay sensitive to them and to keep on loving them. I feel that now, at long last, I can make it with the kids. In my own way, I can reach a few of them with some of Your beautiful truths that I know will bring cheer and comfort to their hearts.

How am I doing, God?

# What Kind of Friend Are You?

There was a woman in our congregation who was about my age, and she had a husband and three children too. There the similarity ended. I had a wonderful, Christian husband who loved me, and our three children were well-fed, well-dressed, happy kids.

Her alcoholic husband beat her and spent most of their money on liquor. If he had any love for her, it had long ago been buried beneath alcohol fumes. Her children were not well fed. They were thin, nervous kids, and their eyes always looked too big for their faces. Their clothes mended hand-me-downs, and they always looked shabby.

I felt sorry for her, and I tried to be her friend. She had a lot of pride — the right kind of pride — and I admired her for that. She and her children came to Sunday school and church, and although they weren't dressed like the others, they were clean and neat, and their heads were held high.

I don't know, of course, how much she gave to the church, but I usually sat in the same pew with her, and I know that she always put something into the collection plate. I used to wonder sometimes about the sacrifice she had to make each week in order to contribute anything at all to the church. Lots of times it made me give a little more.

You could tell that she wanted to be regarded as an equal member of the church. She attended services like everyone else and contributed like the others did. I don't know, maybe it was the one place on earth where she felt she truly belonged.

Her neighbors felt sorry for her, and one or the other of them was always calling the police when her husband became too loud and abusive. They tried, in the only way they knew, to protect her and her children.

At school her children were of the small minority who received a free hot lunch every day.

Clerks in the stores tended to ignore her, to

make her wait until they'd waited on the more prosperous looking women.

I try to imagine how rough it was for her. Still, she never became sniveling. She never held out begging hands. She looked right at a person, and seeing her eyes and that lifted chin, you didn't think of her as poor. She had something else going for her, and it was something to be admired.

I'm sure she had a great faith. That must have been the thing that carried her through each day, the thing that made her able to bear the kind of life she was forced to live.

Like I said, I tried to be her friend. As much a friend as she'd allow me to be, anyway. She wasn't a woman to act grateful because someone like myself acted friendly toward her. There was always a certain wariness about her, as if she were asking, "Are you my friend? Or do you just feel sorry for me? Do you see yourself as Mother Bountiful being nice to the poor? If so, keep away from me. I don't need you."

Over the few years that I knew her, our friendship grew, and she got used to me dropping in now and then. If I'd come over and she'd have a black eye or a new, ugly bruise she couldn't hide, we never mentioned it. We simply acted as though it wasn't there. We were never very close, the way it is with some friends, because she only allowed me to get so close to her and no further. I understood that she was afraid. If she once allowed me to show my pity, all the carefully built walls would collapse.

One night her husband beat her again, only this time he didn't stop until the police arrived. She was rushed to the hospital, and she had to stay there for several weeks.

I seized my opportunity. I brought her children home and gave them the luxury of hot baths and soft beds and three good meals a day. I bought clothes for the boy, and I sewed for the girls.

One day I went to her house and cleaned it. She kept it spotless, but on the night of the beating some things had been thrown around and broken.

I also saw that the walls of the little house, though clean, were ugly. They needed painting, and of course there had been no money for paint. For several days I worked. Blue for this room and a soft gray for that one. A sunny yellow for the kitchen. When I'd finished, I was very pleased with the results.

In a few weeks she came home from the hospital. I was there, with her children, waiting for her. After she'd kissed the children and the greetings were over, she said, "Thanks for taking care of the children." I assured her I'd loved doing it and got ready to leave. Her neighbors, now that the husband was safely in jail, were going to help her for a while. Her eyes flicked over the painted walls. "Thanks again," she said.

I was a little hurt because she hadn't said

anything about the walls. "But then," I told myself, "I'm not much of a Christian if I have to have
thanks for my every good deed."

It was only a few days after that that she
died. The beating had been more than her frail
body could stand.

A neighbor called me, and I dashed over to
the woman's house. We wondered what would
happen now to the children.

"Maybe she has an address book," I said,
"with the name and address of a relative."

After questioning, one of the children mentioned an Aunt Mary.

"Where does Aunt Mary live?" I asked them.

"I don't know. Another place in the world,
I think."

So I rummaged around, feeling guilty, looking for a Miss or Mrs. Mary somebody. Someone
I could call to come and take over.

As I searched through papers in a table
drawer, I came across a black book that looked
like it might be an address book. I opened it. It
was a diary. I flipped to the back pages to see if
any names and addresses were listed there. My
own name stood out in the cramped handwriting
and I read what it said:

"I couldn't quite thank her for painting the
walls, and I'm sorry about that. Oh, well, she
didn't really want to be my friend, anyway. She
was always itching to do her Christian duty
toward me. It stood out all over her. The days

I was in the hospital she was good to my kids and I'm grateful, but why did she have to buy them clothes and sew for them? The kids got the message, and it pointed up how very little we have, how really poor we are. I'm so tired! I'll stop now. *Why didn't she at least ask me what colors I wanted?"*

The last sentence was so heavily underlined the pen had gone through the paper.

I learned something about myself in those next days as I thought and thought about what she'd written. I had spent money and time and effort in order to help her, but all it was was a good Christian deed. I'd thought about it like that, I realized now. I hadn't been her friend, I hadn't given myself to her. I'd always gone to visit her with the idea that maybe I'd find some way to help her. She had been a poor person, a woman who didn't have the material things I had, and I'd pitied her. I had failed to see that if I was truly her friend, if I'd given myself freely, I wouldn't have snatched her dignity, her self-caring, out from under her. I had no right to do that. Why hadn't I cared enough to ask her what colors she'd prefer?

## DEAR GOD . . .

I've been blessed all my life. I've never gone hungry or had to wear shabby clothes. I had parents who loved me and a husband who cherished me.

You know, God, I've always been grateful. Somehow, I have always been aware of how much I had, and I've thanked You over and over. It sounds kind of funny now, but I guess it goes back to my parents always reminding me of the starving Armenians. Actually, they provided me with good things, and they never allowed me to take these good things for granted.

So on that score I'm okay, right? But, as You know, one of my big shortcomings is the fact that I want to play Lady Bountiful. Not that there's anything wrong with that, it's the way I go about it that's not right. Thoughtless. Not thinking about the feelings of the recipient. If I see someone who is in need or doesn't have as much as I have, I want to share my abundance. I want very much to give whatever I can to balance things out a little. My big fault is that I'm a great giver but I don't know how to receive.

Like gratitude, for instance, shown sometimes in obscure little ways. I don't want it, and I forget that I don't have the right to refuse it. Part of my giving must be accepting the gratitude.

And remembering the very real and necessary pride the recipient of my gift has. I certainly don't have the right to step all over that or to ignore it.

I'm beginning to see, Lord, that giving isn't a simple thing. I mean, there is a lot of responsibility that goes with it.

If I just give, without accepting the responsibility that goes with it, then I have this great glow of unselfishness in me, but I haven't given a complete gift. Because I've ignored the dignity of another person. There's a way to help people without trampling all over them and making them feel poorer than before. That's where I need help, God.

The other day my daughter gave me a gift. It was cheap and ugly, God, and something I didn't want. But when she gave it to me, she hugged me and said, "Thanks for everything, Mom." So I cherish that gift because I know why it was given. Help me, dear God, to show my love when I give. Help me to give a part of myself along with the gift.

I very much want a better answer the next time I ask You, "How am I doing, God?"

# Then This Storm Interrupted

A pretty bad thing happened to me a few years ago. Not many people know about it, but there are times when I want to scream out to everyone I know and tell them the truth. I want to tell them why it's like it is for me now. But that only happens once in a while, and I've never given in to that impulse. For the most part I don't want anyone to know anything about it. It's a thing that needs to be buried and forgotten.

I'm not really going to tell about it now except to say that for quite a long time I had just about all the material things a woman could want. Not a chauffeur-driven Cadillac, but we had a nice car and a lovely home, just right for us, and over the long years of our marriage we had accumulated things like silverware and a good set of dishes and pictures and — well, I guess I could go on for hours enumerating the nice things we owned.

Our friends used to remark about our good taste and our lovely furniture and the beautiful things we had sitting on shelves and bookcases.

We liked having these things, of course. We'd worked hard and sacrificed and saved for nearly all of it. But we often reminded ourselves that these things didn't come first in our lives.

"Our faith, the fact of Jesus Christ, comes first and foremost."

"Right! And our children and our health."

"Possessions will never be the uppermost thing in our lives."

We'd tell each other that every single item we owned could be taken from us and we'd still breathe a thank-You to God for what we had left.

Then this storm interrupted and changed everything for me. My husband died, and within a short time something else — someone else — the thing I want to forget — tore into my life and turned it upside down and nothing was ever the same again.

One day there I was, in my car with my children, on a highway headed for someplace. We didn't know where we were going, we only knew we had to get out of that town, never to return, because only evil and hatred and a loaded gun waited there for us.

We had some clothes we'd thrown into the trunk of the car. My daughter had grabbed her radio, and my son thought to take our photograph albums. I'd taken our set of good silverware. My youngest daughter had grabbed her ragged teddy bear, her most precious possession. That's all we had.

Several years have passed now. I've worked, and we've managed. We live in a very small, rented house with the paint peeling off and bare floors that I have to polish so often. It's a humble place we call home now. We have a set of plastic dishes from the dime store and secondhand furniture and handmade curtains at the windows. This Christmas my children gave me a toaster, and I cried. I hadn't realized how much I'd once taken things like that for granted.

All through this very difficult time when I've felt so wrongly persecuted, I've said over and over that my faith has carried me and kept me from being bitter. It's true, I know it, and I've impressed this on my children.

We haven't had any social life to speak of. Not like it used to be. I like to remember the dinner parties we gave. Good food, soft candlelight, background music, all in a lovely, carpeted setting that was ours. Such good times we had, and how I used to love to entertain. It's a happy thing to remember.

Still, I thought I was doing fine. So I had lost everything, and I had to work and struggle a bit. We had a new church home, and I was teaching Sunday school, and my children had new friends. Most important of all, our faith in God was stronger than ever.

Then a person I'd met at work invited us to her home for dinner. It was our first invitation since starting what we called our new life. I'd been in other homes for coffee or a chat at a neighbor's, but in the neighborhood I lived in, the homes were pretty much alike. The paint was peeling off most of them, and fences needed repairing, and garage doors hung loose. Not a bad neighborhood. What they called a middle-class, renters neighborhood.

We drove to my friend's house, and as we approached her street I drew in my breath. There were large, well-manicured lawns with clipped hedges and large trees. The homes were set back from the street, and shiny new cars sat in the curved driveways. "Just like the neighborhood I once lived in," I thought with a pang.

The house was beautiful. Thick drapes shut out the outside, and a fire crackled in the fireplace. My feet sank into deep carpeting that reached out to every corner. My eyes skipped over large paintings on the wall and a silver coffee service and expensive things here and there on tables.

The food was served on good china, and music

from a stereo played in the background. I felt dazed all evening, hardly able to concentrate on the food and conversation.

Driving home, the children were excited. "Wasn't that great, Mom?"

"Wow! I sure enjoyed myself."

"I like her. She's nice."

Finally they noticed that I wasn't saying anything.

"Didn't you have a good time, Mom?"

"You enjoyed it too, didn't you?"

I assured them that I'd had a wonderful time and that I liked our hostess very much too.

"When are we going to invite her to our home for dinner?"

"Yeah. Let's have her over soon."

I said we would, and then we were home and it was late, so I shooed them all off to bed.

I sat up that night—all night long—unable to sleep. Bitterness and anger and jealousy rose up in me and wiped out all possibility of sleep. It wasn't fair for me to have lost all those lovely things! It had never been my fault, and it simply wasn't fair that my very love and unselfishness had been repaid with such hatred. I could never invite my friend to our home. Never! I couldn't stand the comparisons I knew she'd have to make.

For a giddy few minutes I thought of withdrawing my savings and buying some things, but it passed quickly. My meager savings, built up dollar by hard-earned dollar, couldn't begin to buy enough to make a difference.

The next day I was tired and bleary-eyed, and the children asked me what was wrong.

"To tell you the truth, I didn't sleep at all last night."

"Why not?"

I explained my feelings to them. "I'm ashamed of myself," I said, "but I couldn't help thinking about all we've lost and what we have now and — well, it bothered me terribly."

"You shouldn't feel that way, Mom."

"I know. I'm sorry about it."

"You've been telling us how we're supposed to forget the past and be thankful for what we have."

"I know."

"We should just keep on thanking God that we have one another."

"And our health."

"And life."

"I know, you're right. Believe me, it was only a temporary lapse. I'm on the right track again."

"Good! How about inviting her over here next Saturday night?"

"Yeah, Mom. Please invite her."

So I did, and she accepted. I cleaned and waxed and polished. I cooked a good meal. My daughter's record player scratches the music in places, but we turned it down low, and it was pleasant background music. Candles softened some of the cracks in the wall, and we had lively conversation going for us. We didn't apologize for what we had or didn't have. We offered ourselves and our friendship, not our surrounding.

We'll be moving from this house one of these days. My salary has been raised a few times, and my savings account grows steadily. So we'll move to a nicer home, and we're already accumulating a few nice things. Not as many as before, though. Never as many as before, because I know now how unimportant they really are.

I taught my children a good lesson, and I taught them well. I thank God they had the good sense to teach it back to me!

## DEAR GOD . . .

Well, God, You know me. I talk big. But so many times I wonder if I've really learned anything at all. To tell the truth, many times I know I haven't learned very much. I still get little pangs of jealousy when I see a woman getting out of her shiny new car when I'm hoping mine will hold up for just one more year. And I go into a beautiful home and look at the lovely things in it, and I wince just thinking about the things I lost. Some of the women I know go to beauty parlors once a week, and they go on shopping sprees when the mood strikes them. I'd be ashamed to have anyone know what my bank balance is!

Dear Lord, I keep forgetting about my wonderful children and the good health we enjoy. And our happiness always in just being together, and our faith, which is so precious to us. Nothing important has been taken from us.

Am I a snob, Lord? Because I've always had a lot, even though I had to work for it, did I develop into the kind of person who can't be happy without material things?

I don't like to think of myself like that, but maybe it's true.

Still, you'd think I would have learned a little more by this time. I mean, I have proof that I'm wrong! I've stewed and fretted and worried over my finances. More than once. And it wasn't until I gave up and said, "Lord, I'm so tired of it! Take over, please, make it right," that it was all right.

Over and over it's happened like that. So I do need a lot of help. I need to stop thinking about material things. Stop thinking that they're important in any way. I need to settle back and enjoy what I've got and forget about what I don't have. My children do this so easily; why can't I, Lord?

Please help me. I know the serenity and peace that comes with being satisfied with what I've got, and I want that so much!

How am I doing, God?

# Poor Me and My Lonely Island!

Sometimes loneliness has all but overtaken me. As a widow, I've been very lonely: aching for the touch and sound of my husband, finding myself hurrying home with some news to share with him and then realizing that he's no longer here. Sleeping in a narrow, single bed, no longer watching the clock in the evening, listening for his car in the driveway. So many things! He left a deep, lonely hollow inside me, and there are times when I cry for him.

As an author I've known great stretches of self-imposed loneliness. It's absolutely essential for a writer to become familiar with loneliness. We listen to people talk, we record in our minds their tone of voice, how they lift an eyebrow, the way they move their hands when they're angry. We're aware of people and how they react and what they say. But every so often we must crawl to our corner of loneliness and think about all we've observed. Ideas need time to germinate before they can sprout, so the writer forces loneliness upon himself. He's afraid of talking the ideas away, so he becomes a silent, uncommunicative recluse for a time. This kind of loneliness isn't unhappy because something's happening inside. And the knowledge is there that it won't go on forever.

I've known loneliness being with my children. I can't believe that they truly aren't interested in what I'm talking about. I try to get used to the shuffling feet, the eyes darting over to the TV, the tiny polite smiles. I pause for breath, and they gratefully jump in with what they want to tell me. Something happened at school, or a friend is moving away, or they just learned how to roller skate and will I watch. And the lonely feeling creeps in again. My children and I are in the same room with one another, and I'm lonely!

I've been lonely in a crowd, walking down a busy street, shopping in a crowded store. Because I'm part of all the people rushing around me, but I'm not one of them. Sometimes I go shopping, and my mood is happy. I feel a kinship with all my brothers and sisters pushing carts up and down the aisles. Then some little thing happens: A woman accidentally rams her cart into my heel. We stop, she apologizes, I say it's all right, and she pushes on down the aisle. The little exchange puts me back on my island again because her eyes were glazed over with indifference. She was afraid to meet me person to person. She didn't look me in the eye, she looked at her cart, at my heel, muttered an apology out of the corner of her mouth, and rushed away. And then I felt more alone than ever.

Once in a while loneliness makes me feel sorry for myself. Then I remember a woman I met years ago. She was a pastor's wife. Methodist, I believe. Someone said to me, "You should call on her. You'll be glad you did. She's quite a woman."

Curiosity made me go one afternoon. I wondered what there could be about this woman that was so special.

The pastor met me at the door of the parsonage. I introduced myself, and he said, "Come in! She's always glad to have visitors."

I really wondered about this woman now. You'd think she was royalty the way people, including her husband, acted.

I walked into the living room, where she lay in an iron lung, only her head sticking out of the great steel trap.

We talked, exchanged names, mentioned the

weather. Her smile was infectious, and she seemed to be very much at ease.

I had to ask the question. "Are you ever allowed out of . . ."

"My iron lung? No. Oh, for a little time each day I get on that."

She nodded toward the other side of the room. It was a rocking bed.

"My husband straps me in, and away I go for my thrill ride of the day," she laughed.

Then I saw the bulletin board and chalkboard on the wall.

There were brightly colored pictures on the bulletin board, and on the chalkboard some Bible verses had been printed.

"I teach a Sunday school class," she said.

Her husband came in then and told her he was going out for a few minutes.

"Change that tie," she said. "It doesn't go with that suit."

He laughed and shrugged his shoulders. "Okay, anything you say. You're the one with good taste in this family."

Later, one of her children came into the room.

"Have you done your homework?" she asked.

"Sure. I got it all done in a few minutes."

"You'd better bring it here and let me have a look at it."

Then she looked at me, her eyes shining.

"Taking care of a family uses up every minute, doesn't it?" she asked.

I nodded. This woman made me feel ashamed of myself! "You're doing a good job of it," I managed to say.

She shook her head. "I'm only doing what the Lord expects of me," she answered.

Whenever I feel lonely and sorry for myself, I remember that woman and those words. They help bring me up and out of myself in a hurry.

We all have our islands of loneliness, some more than others. Sometimes it seems that I've had more than my share of them. Some have been self-imposed for reasons of my own, and some have been forced on me. The question I ask myself is, What have I done with these times of loneliness? I've raved and ranted through some of them, blaming everyone I could bring to mind. During other times I've allowed myself to dissolve into a teary, mushy blob of self-pity. Seldom have I had the good sense to use them as creative, reflective bonuses.

I remember that dear woman in the iron lung doing what the Lord expected of her, and it helps me a great deal. She refused to let life isolate her on an island of loneliness. She would not allow life to pass her by. She reached out from her confining prison and brought life to herself, and she was very definitely a living, vital part of it. So through her example I've learned that periods of loneliness don't ever have to be miserable, tearful times. Since meeting her I've met others who have made me feel ashamed of myself. A man who lost an arm but continued to work and support his family. I never saw him without a smile on his face. And the man lying in the hospital after a car accident, talking about his wife and eight children at home. Later, after welfare and kind neighbors had helped, smiling and saying, "God always comes through, doesn't He?"

The young woman struggling through the agonizing loneliness of a divorce but forcing herself to bring love and attention to her in-laws.

So many! The list of brave people goes on and on, and I greedily use their examples to set my own heart on the right path. One of these days I'll learn, and then maybe my life can be an example for someone too.

## DEAR GOD . . .

I'm always griping about something! If I'm too rushed and there is too much to do, I come running to You yelling about being imposed upon and asking You if You think it's quite fair.

Then I find myself alone and lonely without enough to do, and I yell about that. I ask You why I have to be so lonely, and please make it better. Like a little child, God!

It's hard to understand why You don't give up on me.

The beautiful, wonderful truth is that You never do!

Well, I need help all the time. Especially about those periods of loneliness I get forced into. I need to think about that dear woman in the iron lung and that one-armed man and the father in the hospital bed.

What I would like, Lord, is to be the kind of person others could use as an example. I'll never make it if I can't learn to stop feeling sorry for myself. With Your help I know I can take any situation at all and turn it into something a little victorious. Help me do that.

Also, help me mature so that I can welcome those little islands of loneliness that drift in and out of my life. Help me see that they can be reflective, creative times for me.

I guess what I really want, God, is to have my self-pity washed away so I can be free to do what You expect of me.

The next time I sit on one of those little islands, I hope I remember in time not to feel sorry for myself. Then I'll be able to smile and look up and ask, "How am I doing, God?"

# You're a Religious Person, Aren't You?

For a time I became fascinated with the truth that all men are my brothers. I mean, I'd always known this, but suddenly I wanted to really practice it. I wanted to go out and embrace the whole world and show everyone how much I loved them. My brothers and sisters in Christ! Everyone—everywhere—I love you! It was a wonderful feeling, and I needed very much to do something about it. I wanted to show the world that I really meant it when I said, "All men are my brothers!"

Then I met a man who was old and disabled, and he drank too much sometimes, and people laughed at him. I looked at him and told myself, "This man is my brother. Maybe he just needs someone to care about him." So with evangelical glee I went to him and talked to him and showed him that I cared. With arms outstretched and a heart full of holy love for my brother, I asked him if he needed me.

He needed me, and at first it was fine, because he was old and disabled, and I was in a position to do many things for him. Yes, it was a fine, Christian thing I was doing, and I never got tired of putting myself out for him, running errands for him, listening to him.

Was I just a little proud of myself? (Oh, say, Lord, look at me! Look at what Your servant is doing!)

I never criticized him or shamed him when he was a little drunk. I didn't sit in judgment, and I noticed eventually that his drinking bouts were becoming less frequent. I thanked God for that! It was surely due to my great Christian love.

I drove him to the store, I drove him home again. My children and I sent happy little notes to him (I finally got around to asking him what his name was). We called him our brother, and it was warm and good. I enjoyed making a cake or a batch of hot rolls for him and seeing the grateful delight on his face.

It was all so wonderful I regretted the years in which I had read and talked and sung about my brothers in Christ but had not experienced the fact of it. It was great — until he started to intrude into my life. He called one day.

"What are you doing?" he asked.

I felt little pricks of annoyance. What business was it of his? "Watching TV" I replied.

Then he wanted to talk to the children. The phone calls came fairly frequently after that. He would always begin by asking me what we were doing, and then he'd ask to speak to the children. I didn't like it at all! This shabby old man had no right to assume that because we'd been nice to him he could intrude into our family life. Just like he was one of our friends or a member of the family. No, I didn't like it. The children, of course, were delighted and started calling him Grandpa. They kept begging me to take them to his house so they could see his cats. I put them off with vague excuses about being too busy. We were not about to make him a member of our family.

I began to dread hearing the phone ring. What right did he have intruding into our lives this way? Wasn't it enough that I took him shopping and baked for him and sent him notes of cheer? Why couldn't that be enough for him? My brotherly love was ebbing away, and I felt put-on.

One day he called again. I told him that I was very busy and had no time to talk. "Also," I added, "the children are doing their homework."

"It's just that my wife is very sick," he said.

Wife? I hadn't known he had one! I'd thought he lived alone with his cats in that little house.

"Your wife?" I asked stupidly. "Where is she?"

"Here, of course," he answered. "With me."

Well, of course! Where else would she be?

"Like I said," he went on, "she's sick. I'm taking her to the doctor."

"I'll take her. I can be over there in a few minutes and . . ."

"No. I already called a taxi. He'll be here in a couple of minutes."

"Oh." I wondered why he'd called me.

"It's just . . . well, I'm not a religious person, you see, but I know you must be." He paused. "You are, aren't you?"

"What? Religious?"

"Yes."

"Well, I'm a Christian, if that's what you mean."

"That's what I mean. A religious person. So I thought — well, you see, I'm really worried about my wife. Will you pray for her?"

"Of course I will! We'll all pray for her. Call me and let me know what the doctor says. You can be sure we'll be praying for her."

I put the phone down. I felt sick! That old man, worried about his wife, frightened, feeling very much alone, had felt a link with me. He had someone to call, to cry out to, to ask for prayers. Because I was a religious person!

I remembered a sermon I'd heard. I could see the pastor, leaning slightly forward, his eyes scanning the faces before him. "God does not want religious people," he'd said, spacing his words. "He wants believers in His Son. Committed Christians. People whose grateful hearts are filled with His kind of love. He doesn't want or need religious people!"

The old man had called me by the right name, I thought. That's exactly what I was: a religious person. I hated the sound of it—the truth of it.

Since then I've learned a little something about being a Christian. About what it really means. For one, I learned that you can't fake it. If it isn't for real, it shows. Anyone can see through a religious person who is going about doing good. It's a very easy thing to say, "You're my brother," and actually think you mean it. But when you start to put that love into action, you must be very careful. My brotherly love doesn't extend so far and wide any more. I'm having quite a time learning about really loving just one brother. It involves so much! Saturday afternoon visits with the children to see the cats. Being patient about a few phone calls. Going to the drugstore for medicine his wife needs. Little things, but I'm learning what love is all about. And I'm gradually getting rid of that tag "a religious person." All men are my brothers, but I'm learning what it means to truly love just one of them.

## DEAR GOD ...

Oh boy, I did it again, didn't I, God? I honestly and truly thought that I had captured the great secret of being a Christian: brotherly love. That's where it was at, and I couldn't wait to go out on the highways and byways and embrace the whole world. You know, I thought of blacks in the ghettos and drug addicts and communists and heathen headhunters, and I loved them all! I wished I could have held them all in my arms.

Why is it, God, that I always seem to have to learn things the hard way? It was a painful thing for me to have to come down from that high pinnacle of self-sacrificing love. To have to come down a long, long way and realize that I was just a religious person and that maybe I felt this great brotherly love for everyone in the world, but my own pride and selfishness were keeping me from really loving just one brother. I guess I was enjoying the picture of me doing good to a less fortunate brother. It was a nice picture, and I was the star. O God, I don't like to think about it!

Thank You for bringing me to my senses. For helping me see that this brotherly love business has to be on a one-to-one basis, personal and real and all of us working very hard at it. I learned something very important, and I've still got a lot to learn.

How am I doing, God?

# What Are They Up To?

There are a lot of people around these days that I don't understand. I'm not used to them; I don't know what they're up to. I guess that's why I haven't been able to believe in what some of them are doing.

In my town there are quite a few young men, neatly dressed, but still with long hair and beards and bare feet, wearing beads and different clothing. They have special houses, some of them, where they meet, which are usually donated to them. They have rattletrap buses they ride around in, and they make the peace sign and talk about Jesus Christ Superstar.

I don't know what they're up to.

I became aware of these young men through two teen-age boys who live on my block. They've been good friends of my son for several growing-up years, and I like them very much. Their parents are divorced, and they live with their mother and sisters just as my son lives with me, his widowed mother, and his sisters.

The boys' mother has done a good job of raising her sons. I know how tough it is, raising a son without a father, and I admired her, but the boys lacked one thing and that was a church life.

I talked to the mother about it. She herself had no particular desire to go to church, she told me, but if the boys wanted to go it was up to them.

"I've always taught my boys right from wrong," she said, "and I've made them live by the Ten Commandments. I think that's good enough."

Of course it wasn't good enough, and I knew it. I asked her if her sons could go to church and Sunday school with us.

"If they want to," she replied.

They were eager to go, delighted that they'd been invited. My son was very happy, and so was I. My only excuse for having waited so long to do it was that I was afraid of offending the boys' mother. I want to win souls for Christ, but I don't want to be too pushy and turn them off before I make any headway.

134

The boys were in the junior high school Sunday school class. Each Sunday, driving home, I'd ask them how it went, did they like it. They always answered that it was okay, yes, they liked it okay. I had the warm, satisfying feeling of having brought two souls to Christ. Great feeling! Maybe they didn't show very much enthusiasm, but then boys that age never do.

Anyway, it didn't last very long. Those long-haired young men with the old bus came around, and pretty soon the boys weren't going to church and Sunday school with us.

"But why not?" I asked my son.

"Because they'd rather go with those other guys."

"I hardly think that's fair."

"Well, they were getting pretty bored at our Sunday school anyway. They just hated to tell you."

"You go to the same class."

"I'm used to it, Mom."

I was puzzled. What did these young men offer that was so much better than we had? What were they up to?

On Sunday mornings, I'd peak out our window from behind the drapes and see this shabby-looking bus in front of the boys' house. They had things like JESUS IS A GROOVE and RIGHT ON WITH JESUS CHRIST painted on the bus. The boys would race out to the bus, their bodies eager, waving their hands, laughing. I noticed they weren't dressed for church. Neat and clean, but wearing blue jeans and T-shirts, and often they were barefooted.

Sometimes on Saturday afternoons too the bus would be there, and the boys would race out, show the peace sign, jump in the bus, and roar down the road.

"Where do they go on Saturday afternoons?" I asked my son.

"Oh, the guys take them roller skating sometimes, and fishing. Things like that."

One day the boys asked me if my son could go with them on Saturday afternoons. I explained that we had a church home. No, my son couldn't go.

"They have a lot of fun, Mom. I sure would like to go with them," my son said later.

"Look, they're what is known as sheep-stealers," I told him. "They only want to take you away from your own church."

My son shook his head. "I don't think so," he said. "They don't even have a church."

I ignored that. My son simply didn't understand. Still, I was jealous of the good times the boys were having with the young men. A boy needs the presence and influence of a man in his life, and it's a hurtful thing to see your son grow up without that needful thing you cannot supply.

Then the boys started going out every Wednesday night too. The old bus always picked them up at seven and brought them home by ten.

"What do you do on Wednesday nights?" I asked one of the boys.

"Oh, just rap about Jesus and the Bible."

"Oh."

I talked to my son again. "Except for the fishing trips and the fun," I said, "what's so much better about their rap sessions than our Sunday school classes?"

"Mom, it is pretty dull in our class."

"It is?"

"Yep. And we always have a woman teacher. I've never had a man teacher in my life. And well, it's a lot of Bible study and memorizing stuff."

I still wasn't convinced. I wondered about those young men and what they were really up to.

One day the boys were in our house, and we talked over milk and cookies.

"Boy!" one of them said. "Exams were sure tough! The older you get, the tougher they get."

"Do you think you passed?"

"Oh, sure! I know I passed."

"How come you're so sure?"

"Well, you see, we were talking about it at one of our rap sessions, and Bill, he's one of the guys, said that I should pray about it. He said I should study hard and pray that Jesus would help me remember the answers. I did study, and I prayed, and Jesus helped me. So I know I passed."

Another time we were talking as I dusted the

furniture, and the boys stood in the doorway waiting for my son.

"You have a nice house," one of them said.

"Thank you. I try to keep it neat and clean, anyway."

"I know. I used to be ashamed of our house."

"You were?"

"Yeah. My mom works, and it's not very neat, and we don't have nice furniture. I really was ashamed of it."

I stopped dusting. "But you're not now?"

"Nope. When we were fishing last Saturday with the guys, we talked about it, and they told us how we don't ever have to be ashamed. Because material things aren't that important. The only thing that really counts is if you have Jesus as your Savior."

"He told us to get busy and help our mother keep it clean, too."

When they'd gone, I sat down and thought for a long time. I was beginning to see what "the guys" were up to. They were bringing Christ to these boys in that ugly old bus. They were bringing Christ into every facet of their lives and showing them how belief in Him is the most important thing in life.

I thought about our church. In our congregation there were a lot of young men; I saw them in church every Sunday. Still, my son had said that he had never in his life had a man for a Sunday school teacher. Why didn't one of them take on a class of boys? A class that included at least one boy who desperately needed his maleness. A man who would show my boy that it wasn't only the women who loved and served the church. How come not one single man in our church ever thought of taking my boy fishing or roller skating?

I really had no idea what my son's teacher did in her Sunday school class, but how dare she bring the Gospel of Jesus Christ to those children and not make it interesting? And relevant? How could she spend an hour a week with them, holding a very precious, exciting truth, and not communicate it to them?

And how could a whole congregation go week after week and not care any more than they did? They didn't need bearded young men or old buses. They had Christian men, fathers and husbands, and they had beautiful cars. Why weren't they doing something to help the boys in our congregation? Also, there are a lot of kids in this town who never go near a church; who never hear about Christ in their homes except when the name is used as a curse. Why don't we all get out and get them? And talk to them and let them see how great it is to be a Christian. We say we believe these things, and we do, but why do we hug it to ourselves?

In my heart, I apologize to those young men in their battered old bus. I wish there was some way I could join them. I will pray for them, and

I will try somehow, some way, with God's help, to make some of the men in our congregation see what they could be doing for Christ.

Anyway, I knew, finally, what those young men were up to.

## DEAR GOD . . .

I guess the big question is what am *I* up to? I mean, I really am concerned about our church and why the men in our church don't do more than they are doing. For You, dear Lord. They have so much to offer, but most of them act like just going to church on Sunday is enough. And of course, it isn't. They drive up to church in their late-model cars, in their conservative, neat suits, with shined shoes and clean hands. Their hair is not too long, and they're clean-shaven. They sit in church with their pretty wives and beautiful, slightly spoiled children, and I suppose they're a little satisfied with themselves.

I look at them and see all that they have to offer. Boys in the Sunday school would surely welcome a man teacher. Fatherless boys would be overjoyed! It would be nice for fatherless girls too.

I've heard these young men talk about the Jesus Freaks, and I know they feel as I once did. "What are they up to?" they ask.

Like I said, God, the question is, What am *I* up to? I feel the need, the importance, and what I need to do now is think about this and see if there isn't something I can do about it.

Please help me! Give me some ideas. Show me some ways to reach these young men in our congregation so that they can see how desperately they're needed.

The next time we talk about this, God, I hope I can expect a good answer from You when I ask, "How am I doing, God?"

# A Black Widow Is a Bothersome Thing

As a widow I was a mess! A black mess. My mood, my attitude, my outlook were all black. Not my clothes. I didn't care enough about my appearance to dress in widow's black. Any old thing was good enough. Who cared anyway what I looked like? Nobody. Certainly not me.

I twisted my hair up in an unattractive bun; I gained weight; my face was glum, and my eyes were sad. My shoulders had the weight of loneliness and self-pity perched on them, and I preferred to sit alone in my shadowed corner.

I told anyone who would listen that nothing mattered to me any more except my children and my church. There wasn't very much joy in it, but I kept very busy concentrating on church and children. I worked hard and told myself over and over that I was doing the right thing. Life was over for me. It had ended at the moment my husband drew his last earthly breath. But I could do some good through my children and my church and not waste the years I had left. Of course, those years left to me were to be waiting years. My husband and I would meet again in a better world.

I frightened my children with the intensity of my devotion to them. I never let them alone, free to make their own mistakes. I was devoting my life to helping them, caring for them. Nothing was too much for me to tackle. After all, I didn't have a life that mattered, so everything was for my children.

I worked so hard in the church that I was criticized. I taught Sunday school, I served on the board of parish education, I taught two adult Bible classes, and I was active in the women's organizations. I worked for every luncheon, supper, picnic, or special meeting they had. A few people thought this was madness and whispered about it behind my back.

That's the way it went for a long time. The bustling activity, the concentrating, helped to ease the terrible loneliness, and I didn't leave myself time to sit down and admit how much it hurt. I was very brave and unselfish and, I suppose, a little proud of myself for being so brave. I never realized for a minute how pitiful I was. Nobody told me.

But I had a friend who helped me in many ways. It was through her that I came to know what the term "communion of saints" is all about. She showed me that we are like-minded people trying together to be little Christs. She taught me that we should bring our fears and worries and burdens to one another. We are supposed to take these things that weigh us down and lay them on our brothers and sisters in Christ. And each, as the occasion presents itself, is to pick up that weight and so distribute it and make nothing of it. At the very least, dissipate it.

Anyway, my friend helped me take the first steps back to a normal life. She did many things and spoke very frankly to me. Sometimes she made me laugh, and other times she reduced me to healing baths of needful tears. The main thing is, she cared about me very much.

One of the things she did was to force me to see what a ridiculous, pitiful thing I had become. She was quite subtle about it, but it worked very well.

She told me one day of a woman she'd met. "She's really a black widow," she commented.

"A black widow?"

"Yep! All dark and black and feeling sorry

for herself. She cries all the time and complains about her health and her loneliness."

"Poor thing!"

"Sure, but people are getting sick and tired of her. She can't go to church any more because the funeral service was held in that church and she says, 'I keep seeing his casket!'"

"Well . . ."

"The thing is, people feel sorry for her, of course, but it's about time she started acting like a Christian. You can't go on mourning your dead forever. After while, it just becomes a selfish preoccupation."

"Why do you call her a black widow?"

"Oh, she's just like the spider. Scuttling around in her dark corners. And she carries a little pouch of self-pity that she'll squirt all over you if you get too close." She stopped and then added, "I'll tell you, these black widows are bothersome things!"

My friend gave me some food for thought that day. I wasn't too sure how much she knew about spiders, but she certainly had people pegged correctly.

Another time my friend persuaded me to go to a luncheon at another church. She knew a lot of the women there and introduced me to some of them. Later, she asked me if I recalled meeting one woman in particular.

"The one in the big red hat," she said.

Yes, I remembered.

"Another black widow. She's the helpless type. Right after her husband died, she suddenly lost any skills she'd had. She calls people and asks them to take her shopping, and she wonders very loudly about how she's going to get her lawn cut. She can't do anything for herself any more, and she puts on her poor, helpless widow face, and, well, she goes begging."

My friend shook her head. "I'm getting so tired of these women!" she said. "These black widows are bothersome things."

The message finally sunk into my brain. I started comparing myself to these black widows my friend told me about, and at first I was able to assure myself that I was nothing like them. Then, as I thought more about it and looked at myself and what I was and what I'd once been, I began to see the truth. And I didn't care much for the truth.

I went to my friend. "I've become a black widow, haven't I?" I asked her.

She put her arms around me. "You sure have, my friend!" she replied.

"Okay," I said, "you've shown me what I am. Now show me how to change."

"That's easy. Come on out from your dark corner. Join the human race again. Think about yourself."

"Why?" I asked, and the question came from my very depths. Right where I lived. "Why?"

And then my dear friend explained, and

though she didn't put it in those words, it was all about the ecology of me. About the fact that I had no right as a Christian woman to bury myself and try to hide from the world. I had no right to gather my children and my church to my dark bosom and ignore the fact that there was a world outside with people in it. Jesus said to go into the world, to be in it but not of it. But most certainly to be a living, vital part of it.

I learned something important about being a Christian woman. It's rather an easy thing to sit in the church fellowship hall and nod your head and agree to send money to missionaries in New Guinea. Then, with your money, someone can do the job of spreading the Gospel of Jesus Christ. It's not so easy to go into the world ourselves and show the face of Christ. It's not always a simple thing to be in the world, and one of God's people, not set apart and different, but one of them, like them, with the glorious difference of having Christ. And then to show the world that His way is the best way and that He is not confined to the church. He lives in His people. He is always where the people are, where they need Him the most. Sometimes we feel superior about being a churchgoer, but if our Christ is confined to the church, we're on the wrong track.

That's how I stopped being a black widow. I remember too well how it was and how I couldn't see the world too well or hear what God's people were talking about. The hurt and the loneliness are still there, somewhere deep inside me, but I don't advertise it any more. Through prayer, Christ has eased the pain, and I'm able to bear it. It's such a relief, because now I can be about the important business of being a little Christ, not a black widow, who can be such a bothersome thing!

## DEAR GOD ...

You know what, God? When I look at it in retrospect, I realize that I enjoyed my misery! I really enjoyed it! You knew that, didn't You?

At first, the fact of my dear one's death sent me crashing into a state of shock. Then it was so easy to stay there, in the darkness, and feel sorry for myself. It was painful to even think about being a whole person again.

It's terrible now to realize how much I enjoyed wallowing in my misery. I'm thankful it's over!

So, God, I'm on the right track now, and that dark, depressing time is over. The thing I want to thank You for is my friend. We read and talk and sing about Christian love, but she is love, isn't she? She's love personified. She taught me such an important, precious truth. Thank You, God, for sending her to me. I know now what the communion of saints is all about. I see how beautiful it is that we can go to one another, in love, and pick up one another's burdens. We can confess to one another and help one another and have a great deal of love for one another.

Being a Christian is more than worshiping together and working on committees together and teaching one another's children. It's a vital, beautiful communion of saints loving one another.

My friend taught me that, God, and I'm so grateful. Help me, please, to never forget this important truth.

How am I doing, God?

# Other Times-Other Places

There have been other times. Times when I've asked, "How am I doing, God?" knowing the answer had to be a negative one. Sometimes my life brushed ever so briefly with the life of another, and still, even in that little episode, I managed to forget so many of the important things. Like you don't always have to offer a ten-course meal to someone to prove your love. Sometimes, the offer of a cup of coffee and a few minutes' companionship will suffice. Maybe that's all that's wanted. It isn't always after the big, earthshaking events that we stop and ask God how we're doing. The little things pile up day by day, and sometimes it becomes important to ask about them too. Together, they form a fairly large picture.

I think of the time one long-ago summer when I worked as a waitress. It was the first and last time I'd been a waitress, and I did it to make enough money to buy a secondhand car. I told the restaurant manager that of course I'd had experience doing waitress work. My lie was discovered the first day. I couldn't carry plates of hot food on my arm, because my skin was not toughened by years of carrying hot plates that way. I didn't know I wasn't supposed to keep filling a customer's glass with tea. Things like that.

Nevertheless, I wanted that car, so I worked very hard. In time, the boss complimented me and even asked me to stay on when the summer was over. The thing that I can't forget is the way I looked down on the other waitresses. The ones who did that kind of work for a living. I was always very quick to let everyone know that I didn't work as a waitress for my living. It was a job, believe me, that I could handle, but I certainly didn't have to do it to eat three meals a day or keep a roof over my head. I gave the impression that it was work that was beneath me and only something I'd do for a little extra money. I believed it too, and I didn't care what the other waitresses thought of me. It didn't occur to me to stop and ask, "How am I doing, God?" I was doing fine!

I quit at the end of that summer, and I had enough money to buy a secondhand car, and I was quite pleased with myself. However, I've learned a few things since those days, and I marvel at my own audacity. Since when is any honest work a thing to be sneered at, looked down on? Certainly we can serve God, no matter what our vocation. I'd like to be able to apologize to those waitresses for my attitude. But one thing: I've never looked down on any honest work since that time.

During the years in which I worked as a secretary, I became highly critical of the younger girls who seemed to be so lazy. They were unsure of themselves, took long coffee breaks, and they couldn't even spell, for crying out loud! I could have been more patient with them and tried to help them, but instead I let them know that I didn't approve of them. If they couldn't work as hard as I did, I wanted no part of them. I was older and more experienced, and my bosses appreciated me, and so the young ones had to do pretty much as they were told. I look back now and wonder why I was so thoughtless. Surely those girls couldn't have liked me very much or enjoyed working with me! If I could live that period over, I'd be more understanding about their youth and their inexperience, and I'd try to help them.

Once I was a pastor's wife. Then my husband entered the military chaplaincy, and I became an army wife. Which was fine, but I found myself shuddering away from any religious activity that wasn't Lutheran.

"A general Protestant service? What's that? Maybe I can find a Lutheran church not too far from the base."

"The Protestant Women of the Chapel? Is that all they are—just non-Catholic?"

"Me teach in the Protestant Sunday school? Sure! I'll give them Lutheran doctrine up to their little ears!"

I believed in the Lutheran teachings with all my heart, but I can't imagine now why I thought I couldn't worship God with a general Protestant congregation! Since those foolish days, I've known and worked with and loved people of every faith. A priest, a rabbi and his wife, a Southern Baptist couple—they are all numbered now among my dear friends. The memory of my first weeks as an army wife are ones I keep quiet about as much as possible!

Being a pastor's wife wasn't always a bed of roses. Still, I know that I complained too often. Sometimes when I'd get together with other pastors' wives, our main topic of conversation was how rough a life it was, how we never had any privacy, how overworked our husbands were, and how unappreciated we were. Then we'd laugh and say, well, in spite of it, we wouldn't change anything, and it really was a good life after all. We just had to let off steam once in a while. Nothing wrong with that!

But I did complain too often, and I should have been down on my knees every day thanking God for the very special privilege that was mine. Now that I'm just the widow of a pastor, and out of it, I'd give a lot to have those old worries back. The ones I complained about then, but I wouldn't now.

Finally, I haven't had many opportunities to show how I feel about the racial problem. I know that my heart cries with and for all black people because of what's been done to them for so long. I know that they are my brothers and sisters even though right now not very many of them want to accept me. I know I pray always for peace and love between us, for the stupid hatreds to be washed away. Still, I don't go out of my way to show them I love them. I learned the hard way not to do that!

I know that I've been disappointed in myself when I've heard others talk against them, their prejudices controlling their tongues, and I've said nothing. Feeling as I do and claiming to be a Christian, it's been a terrible thing for me to remain silent in the face of prejudice. When it comes to this, I hate to ask God how I'm doing!

There have been so many ways in which I've shown my unlovely self. I could write on and on, page after page, enumerating all those times

155

when there couldn't be a good answer to my question "How am I doing, God?" Still, I've learned from those times, and I'm trying, daily, to improve. I'm trying to be the kind of Christian woman I want so desperately to be. I suppose I'll be trying, and making mistakes, and learning, up to the day I die.

The comforting fact I hold close is that God understands. He forgives and forgets, and He lets me start each day over again. I'm afraid I'll never be the complete Christian woman I want to be. My human frailty will always prevent this, but I glory in the truth that God loves me. Not because of what I am, but in spite of it. For that reason I'll never be afraid to ask, "How am I doing, God?"

# Why I Wrote This Book

There is a lot of talk nowadays about what a woman is. Is she a sex symbol, born and raised for the pleasure of man? Put here only to bear and raise his children? The TV and magazine ads tend to make us think this is true. They tell us how to paint our faces, color our hair, perfume our bodies so that we can attract and keep a man. They tell us that if we use a certain brand of flour or coffee or buy certain cleaning products, we will be better housewives, pleasing our men and making them want to come home to us. It would be rather easy to believe that if our floors don't gleam, if our clothes aren't super white, and if the meals we put on the table aren't perfect, our man will not care to come home to us. We can consider ourselves a dismal failure as a woman. We could be uptight all the time if we believed this was true.

We Christian women are concerned about what our role is. Are we secondary creatures created by God to catch a man, raise his children, and follow him meekly to the grave? Reading the Bible doesn't help much if we concentrate on the Old Testament and some of the things Paul had to say about the status of women in the New Testament. However we know that times have changed, and whether or not we've really come a long way, baby, we are very much concerned about our status as Christian women.

There is one thing we can be sure of, regardless of what our attitude is toward all this rumbling and arguing: it is that we know you can't classify us. You cannot put us in a pigeonhole of your mind and say, "That's what a woman is!" Because we are many things, and our roles change and shift like the sands of the beach. We have many roles in life: daughter, sister, career girl, wife, mother, grandmother, widow, to name some of them. The important thing to us is not what we are at a certain moment of our lives but how we're doing as a woman, in relation to God.

We ask the question over and over all through our lives: "How am I doing, God?" At one time, we want to be the best daughter possible, another time, a loving wife, and a good mother. We're constantly striving for the best, trying to keep our goals as lofty as possible.

The secret part of a woman longs for a right relation to God above everything else. As she walks through life in her various roles, striving, sometimes failing, sometimes triumphant, this very private part of her stops and asks, "How am I doing, God?" and she cares very, very much about the answer to her question.

This book is for all the women who ask that question and care about the answer. It's a conglomerate of experiences familiar to all women. Through the telling of one woman's numerous failings I hope there can be meaning for many. We can think of ourselves, dredge up memories of our own actions and feelings, and then ask, "How am I doing, God?" Self-reflection should be an important thing in every woman's life. Through our mistakes and our unlovely ways we can learn, and although our answer sometimes to "How am I doing, God?" will be: "Not so good, Lady!" we can hope and pray that the next time the answer will be: "Well done!"

That's what this book is about. Women of great faith, women of no faith; women who love gossip; women who have known tragedy; women who have loved a man; women who have raised children, had a friend, been betrayed, lost a love, known disappointment—women. Read, and see yourself. Glory in the times when you handled a like situation so much better; cry with me when you too showed your unlovely self. Hopefully, learn what a complex, wonderful, fearful, and all-consuming thing it is to be a whole woman. One who walks with God and so often finds it necessary to stop struggling and go alone to her closet and quietly ask, "How am I doing, God?"